Finding Home at Lilac Hill

Joan D. Cooper

ISBN 978-1-68206-013-3

Library of Congress Control Number 2014930921

Published by Salt Water Media
29 Broad Street, Suite 104
Berlin, MD 21811
www.saltwatermediallc.com

Cover Art: Photography by Stella Cunningham
Interior Book Art: Paintings by Tim Cooper

ACKNOWLEDGEMENTS:

Many thanks to friends who read drafts for this and other ventures—Katherine, Amber, Kathryn, Mary Jo, Ashley and Kim. Special thanks to Dorothy and her reading group. To my daughter Becca, thanks for the laughter, road trips and advice.

ACKNOWLEDGMENTS

[faded, largely illegible text]

PRELUDE

Lilac Hill

The little farm perched on the southern slope of Lilac Hill stared at the trucks passing miles away on the old state road. A modest, two-story Victorian with aged white trim and faded blue shingles faced the drive that wound around a large gray boulder anchored into grass that was once edged a field of shielding corn. The twin ruts of the drive had slowly filled with grass and leaves for the ten summers the farm had lain fallow. The fields that spring were lush with tall grass, the pink tips of wildflowers and yellow honeysuckle from vines twining at the wood's edge. The trees bordering the vacant fields leaned toward the farm as if to reclaim it. Encroaching saplings predicted it. One still-defined trail head beckoned even from five miles away where traffic raced down to Charleston or north to Wheeling.

The farm nestled into itself and waited. The homestead had been visited last by two sisters. The younger woman had painted "Monroe Farm at Lilac Hill" on a board from the corn house that had been gone for generations. The fading signpost emblazoned the name on the porch post and repeated in white letters on the mailbox. Swallows nesting under the eaves of the vacated front porch waited for the Monroe sisters to return and claim their quiet home.

Julie Leaves for Lilac Hill

April Fool's Day was a good day to change your life. Juliet Monroe Elliott rose early and threw the last of her pantry into boxes. She looked around the shabby townhouse she'd rented with her husband in the scrubby complex outside Wheeling. She ate a bowl of cereal after loading the car to the gills and mulled over this move for one more, nervy minute.

She'd called the rental manager and told him that he could sublet the place by the end of the week. Last night, she had quickly packed all of her husband's belongings in boxes she picked up every day for a week from the supermarket. Michael's underwear and sock drawers were in a pickle box, his CD collection in a soup box, and his tools were a jumble in boxes marked "consumable," "fragile" and one very sturdy orange crate that she had been tempted to keep. She hadn't cried because she feared she'd never stop if even one drop tore loose from her abused tear ducts.

When her husband's friend Walt stopped by to pick up all of the boxes, the big man stood in the doorway for many minutes rubbing his forehead. "The police still have no leads? I can't believe he'd just disappear like that on his own."

She had shaken her head and picked up one of the lighter boxes she could manage. "Walt? I think he doesn't want to be found." She sighed, "His mom and I had it out over it. She says Michael told her he was frustrated with us. That the bills and the kids were too much pressure." The tension with her in-laws had grown since her husband's disappearance.

Walt nodded and picked up the box of tools with a grunt, "A move to that farm of yours might be good. My mother and father live right in town. I still live just outside Lambertville. It's a friendly place. What do your cousins think about you moving out to the country?'

Julie swallowed bitterness, "Walt, I've burned some bridges. They all think I'm crazy, but I need a new start." Moving to the little farm was her only recourse. She couldn't continue to pay the credit cards, the rent and utilities while buying food for four. The farmhouse might be decrepit, but the place came rent free.

When her father died, there had been enough funds in his bank account for his funeral and her sister's next semester at Boston University. His retirement account had been depleted by Julie's costly divorce and the purchase of the farm. They'd been surprised by his purchase of a property in rural West

Virginia. Neither of the sisters could remember their father traveling any further than Wheeling when his cousins hosted reunions at their big house. Their mother had been drawn to the little farm carved out of a hillside well off the main road through that part of the state.

The deed had arrived a few weeks after their father's death and had needed only their signatures to transfer ownership. Sarah had returned to college, and Julie had accepted a job transfer to a town outside of Pittsburgh. They had considered the farm an odd inheritance from their father. After they sold the family home in Trenton, the sisters had moved the remains of their childhood home to Lilac Hill. With Julie's two small children, they had enjoyed one quiet summer at the farm grieving their father and trying to make sense of the investment. They had searched for a letter, a journal entry or card that would explain why their father would cash in his investments and buy a piece of property they remembered from a few trips when they were children. They knew their mother's family had once lived in the area, but there was no family left in Lambertville, forty miles south of Wheeling and nestled between two round top mountains. Neither sister had discovered the reason their dependable and wise father would have bought the property near a town he had never visited.

Julie often wondered if any decision she made was wise. When she was lucid, she thought she might have married Michael while heart-sore after her father's sudden death. She had met Michael at her cousins' place in Wheeling two months after the funeral and had married Michael Elliott before that year ended.

Life presented a series of blind purchases, whether it was a house, a car or a husband. The farm outside Lambertville might be mortgage-free, but the house was outdated and worn. She had little reserve cash for repairs and all of their credit cards were spent to the limit. Walt had suggested applying at the coal mine which was barely twenty miles south of the rural state road that passed the farm. She had called and arranged an interview for a bookkeeping position, so the move out to the country was a plausible solution.

Her new life in Wheeling, West Virginia had gone from a hokey romance right out of a dime-store novel to a real-life tragedy in three brief years. She looked back on meeting Michael, their first dance and their whirlwind courtship that resulted in a baby daughter and a hurried wedding. Their relationship had been relaxed until the bills mounted, and Michael decided that driving a cross-country, truck route was the best way to battle poverty. The driving contract brought in more money, but the added income was off-set by the loan on a new rig, insurance and traveling expenses. Julie had married Michael during the first flush of love, but she was a moody woman with three children. Julie had often thought it was a miracle they'd lasted through arguments and silences fueled by time apart for work.

On April Fool's morning, she woke the children and put on her best brave face, "Come on, sleepyheads. We're going off on adventure." Julie remembered her mother introducing the trips they took every summer like that. The little farmhouse at Lilac Hill stood for escape, and escape was exactly what Julie needed.

In a fit of temper the previous week, she'd quit her job. The bank manager had asked her into his office and said that the sympathy from Michael's disappearance had worn thin; she would have to work her usual hours. One of the other account managers had made a snide comment that sounded just like the bank manager's warning, and Julie had bristled into rage. After she resigned and packed her desk in a paper bag, she couldn't get her hands to stop shaking. She wanted Michael back; she truly missed her father; she considered calling her sister but stopped halfway through the call.

Then Julie had screamed at her mother-in-law who stopped by unannounced because no one had answered the phone in days. The woman's narrowed eyes at the piles of dishes in the sink, and the damning evidence of disarray in the house irritated Julie to breaking point. Michael's mother offered to take the children home until Julie got herself together, so Julie asked her to leave.

The visit from the deputy in charge of her original missing person's report was the final trial. He offered a report from Utah and a phone number for her to call later. She broke down while trying to speak to the police detective from Utah who said that Michael's truck had been found abandoned at a truck stop. The cab had been cleaned out, and the tags had been removed and turned in to the state motor vehicle department through a drop box. They tracked the truck down to Michael's missing person status from the serial numbers. Michael Elliott had disappeared.

The officer warned that the truck was running up storage fees, so Julie called the trucking company. Julie battled panic over the payments on the truck. She called the loan company and told them that Michael was missing. She didn't care what they did to the rig because she couldn't afford to do much more than buy groceries and cover the rent. Michael had fallen off the planet, and it didn't look like he wanted to be found. The empty leads made her heart ache. She gave the loan company the address of the tow lot and sent a notarized statement turning possession back to them. She felt bankruptcy looming.

Julie filled up the station wagon with everything she could, gave away some of the excess furniture to neighbors and paid the guy two doors down to paint every room. She figured the security deposit would get her through another month at the farm.

The security deposit never arrived. Julie collapsed after partially unpacking into late mornings and haphazard cleaning. The house, the huge yard, barns and woods were daunting with the children wandering away. She found herself in a daze most of the time because she slept so little. She took the office job at the coal mine and accepted help that Walt or his parents arranged. She could hardly afford to pay the teenage babysitters who did nothing but watch TV and sleep on the couch. The house went from barely ordered to jumbled and then quickly morphed into chaos.

Walt brought her groceries one evening and asked, "Have you told your sister that you've moved?" He'd noticed that all the mail had been forwarded from Wheeling. Birthday cards for Annabelle hadn't even been opened. "I would think your sister could help you out for a while." When Julie began to cry, he brought her the phone and helped her find Sarah's number.

Walt Stone left Monroe Farm one evening in mid-May, but he hesitated at the top of the rutted drive. He'd stepped through the piles of clutter in the kitchen and scrounged to feed the children that evening. After he was sure the children knew where to look for their next meal, he'd tried again to get Julie to call her sister, her mother-in-law or one of her cousins. He tapped on his steering wheel and considered returning to the Monroe house and taking the children home. He worried that he should call the authorities. He cursed Michael Elliott's absence. He drove straight to his parents' home in Lambertville. That evening Walt and his parents decided to intervene one more time before they called the county social services agency.

CHAPTER 1

Waking at Monroe Farm

"Birds? It must be birds." Sarah Monroe forced her eyes open but narrowed them to listen to the fluttery scratching that had woken her. Mice had been the first thing she conjured, but the chirps did not forecast vermin. The tiny, first floor bedroom off the kitchen offered a front porch window and constant shade from the long extended roof that was partially screened. She stood and stretched cramped muscles from all the driving and work yesterday. Peering out the window and straining to see the corners of the high porch ceiling, Sarah found the nest from the debris scattered down the wall and poking out from a crook of beams. She waited until she saw beady eyes peering back at her and smiled. Some kind of field bird then.

She rolled her shoulders and gazed the woods creeping up on the house. At twilight last night, she'd pulled a chair out to the porch to gaze at the bright stars and worry over the woods advancing on the once-defined fields. Their little farm on Lilac Hill was a derelict wreck instead of a sanctuary like she had remembered it.

Sarah unpacked another suitcase and shook out her best dress. She worried that it was too fancy for a church service in Lambertville, West Virginia. The light green silk would also be considered dressy in Boston, but she shrugged and tossed it over her head. She had intended to wear it under her graduation robes at the commencement ceremony that she missed yesterday. She looked in the mirror and practiced a brave face that she wanted to show the children and her sister. Sarah grimaced at her reflection because she saw the jitter of bad nerves in her narrowed eyes, the tightly pressed lips and the arch of her dark brows.

When Sarah had returned home from work on Thursday night, there had been a long teary message from Julie asking for a call back at a new phone number. Returning the call on Friday morning, she had caught Julie in the middle of a crying jag. Pacing in the staff break room at the restaurant, Sarah had silently listened as Julie confessed that she had moved to their Lilac Hill farm because everything in Wheeling had gone sour.

Julie's voice cracked with distress, "Michael has been missing for months, but his truck was found abandoned in southern Utah. I've called the trucking company to see if they could get it out of impound. The daily storage fees are ridiculous." She bit back another sob and added, "I cosigned for it. The checking account he had for the business is nearly empty, and the last debits were made in another state two weeks before he disappeared. There are no other leads." Sarah had stopped pacing to listen for what hadn't been said.

"Why didn't you call me? Why call me now? I expected the five of you for the commencement ceremony tomorrow. What is going on at the farm?" Sarah hadn't been told Michael was missing, but it was the pitch of distress in her sister's voice that alarmed her. When Julie said nothing, Sarah continued, "What about Michael's family and our cousins?"

Julie sounded pouty, "I'm not going there right now, Sarah. Is it too much to ask you to take a few weeks off and help me? You were planning on staying for a few weeks in June, weren't you?"

Sarah had intended to beg off the trip because she had just been awarded the position at the restaurant. She had been looking forward to showing her family Restaurante Majorane and the neighborhood she imagined moving into after graduation. All those plans blew away like dust as Sarah imagined Julie alone with her three children on the large farm. Though the property was beautiful in the summer when they visited, the house was so dilapidated that they'd dubbed their time there "camping at Monroe Farm."

Sarah concluded that Julie must be grieving Michael as she faced mounting bills and no real support system. Sarah didn't need to speculate on the topic of the argument with Michael's family. Just as Sarah decided to call their older cousins in Wheeling, Julie had broken into her thoughts, "I took an accounting position at the mine, but there's a better job. I'd work the five to three shift. I can start the job on Sunday morning, but there is no sitter, and things are bad."

"Five to three during the day doesn't sound bad," she stated with her heart sinking. Sarah understood that phrase, "Things are bad."

"Not daytime, Sarah. The night shift. You know, overnight? I need somebody to live here. You're off for the summer, aren't you?" Julie couldn't take that job without someone living with them at the farm. Panic clutched at Sarah's chest and wormed into her belly. "Can't you come and help me get back on my feet?

Julie had calmed and droned on as Sarah's gut clenched into a knot. In a generous but ill-timed reflex, the trucking company had agreed to retrieve the truck and hire another driver for the present if Julie continued partial payments on the new rig. She had agreed to their offer for six months, hoping her husband could be found. Financially strapped, she struggled with frustration, and panic bubbled in her disjointed explanations. Julie sniffled, hiccupped back into sobs, and finally begged Sarah to come to live with her again.

Sarah hadn't called for all that. Julie always called crying over some tragedy. Sarah originally called back to see if she needed to hold the five tickets she'd saved for the commencement ceremony. She'd wanted to tell Julie that she'd just been offered a full-time assistant position at the restaurant, and that she had achieved summa cum laude in her graduate degree. She'd half-known that Julie's promise to attend the ceremony wouldn't be kept like so many other pledges. She'd half-known that something would topple Sarah from the slow ascent she'd been climbing.

They'd been stuck in this pattern all their lives; Julie would need help and expect it while Sarah could only depend on herself. Julie would be broken down, depressed and need rescue. Sarah experienced crippling panic attacks, but she had learned to handle the pressure alone.

Sarah wasn't too puffed up over the graduate degree; she was more eager to keep her new position at a Boston restaurant under Chef Jennings' direction. He appeared to the world as an imposing dictator with entrenched routines and screaming fits over idiosyncratic details. He reminded her over and over that she was a "babe in the woods" or "dilettante of cookery" with her back door culinary arts degree. Sarah shrugged over how she'd arrived at her station. She had been ecstatic to be hired after a tumultuous internship at Majorane, Jennings' flagship eatery.

She ended the phone call with her sister and returned to work but fainted a few hours later when a wrenching attack of stomach pain hit her tense body. Despite his habit of biting off the heads of all bearers of bad news, Chef Jennings took Sarah out for a slow walk around the block, gave her a handkerchief for her tears and time off to take care of the emergency. He listened to her worries over the children, her sister and the last doctor's visit when she was given a stronger prescription and the advice to slow down.

David Jennings patted Sarah's back and soothed, "I will hold your position at Majorane for a week. If you must stay longer, you may return to one of my restaurants when you return from your 'little vacation.' I'm sure this missing husband will return." He avoided asking about Sarah's doctor's visit or her health. Life in the restaurant was not without drama or pressure. He looked at pictures of Sarah's sister and the three children, listened to the description of their little farm retreat in West Virginia, and directed, "Write down the address, so I can send your final check. I'll give you a bonus to help with travel expenses."

Sarah finished her shift and packed her apartment as she fought the onslaught of regret and foreboding. Her roommate had been hinting that her brother needed a place to stay in the city. Another chef could be hired in her place at Majorane, and Georgie's brother might move into her room at the apartment. Unlike other trips when she set out knowing she would be back, there was bitter taste in Sarah's mouth. She packed her tiny hatchback with anything she thought she'd need for a few weeks and boxed up the rest. The rush of her graduate classes, the demanding schedule at the restaurant and her hectic social life with Georgianna had ended with one phone call.

Early on that first morning at Lilac Hill, Sarah stretched as she looked out on the mountain that the map called Lilac Hill. The steep slope was lushly forested with little paths from animals that led to the crest on their side of the hill. Yesterday evening, she had hiked up beyond the property line with the children and looked out on the valley to view the farm and the strip of woods that divided their property from the larger working farm to the south. From a distance, Monroe Farm appeared a smallish place with four outbuildings including a small, two-floor caretaker's cabin, toolshed, barn and mechanical shop. The leftover patchwork of six fields had been tilled and planted when she visited as a child. The main house faced the valley with five bedrooms, one, huge bath and an aged kitchen. Open porches ran the length of the front and back of the house. From the top of Lilac Hill, the back of the main house didn't look as shabby or worn as it was. With the weathered, wooden siding repainted, Sarah imagined the house might look quaint, perched on its flagstone foundation.

Since it was Sunday morning, Sarah woke her nephew and two nieces early and told them to wash their faces, brush teeth and dress in their best clothes. She was not a particularly religious person, but Sarah understood that some benevolent spirit had allowed her worn hatchback to safely make the trip from Boston. Her roommate had kicked the tires and complained about the tired, little vehicle that Sarah rarely drove.

Glancing at the academic robe in the closet, Sarah imagined the pomp and circumstance that would have closed her long, college career and her life in Boston. She gazed at the farm clinging to the side of the mountain and regretted leaving her job with Chef Jennings and the rest of the staff. She'd been replaced so easily. She considered the stone foundations of all of the buildings and mused over permanence in this small place.

Stepping over teetering mounds of clothing, boxes and toys, Sarah frowned. Some sense must be made out of Julie's formless habits. Temporary fixes like this one did not solve problems. Julie's reactions to stress were more like applying a finger bandage to a gaping wound. After spending one day at the farmhouse, Sarah had been impressed with its whirlwind of chaos and near hysteria. The children had few clean clothes, the pantry had been nearly empty, and the grass around the house was knee high. Minimal survival had become the order of the day. Julie's eyes were glazed with pain, and the children were confused about the recent move, Michael's absence and the daily schedule. There was no daily schedule.

Julie and Sarah had always attended weekly services at home in Trenton with their parents. Sarah had driven through town early on Saturday morning and had counted two churches: a small Methodist building with the prerequisite red door and the white Lutheran Church with its traditionally tall spire closest. The Lutheran Church was closest to the farm which was over ten country miles outside of town. Julie had been married in her husband's home parish in Wheeling, and he was Lutheran. Sarah shrugged and decided to attempt the white spired church as the closest thing to her native Catholic as she could find. Sarah thrived on quiet and clock-like order. Sunday worship was a time for reflection once a week, and attendance built a sense of community. She thought the children might need that connection, too.

Sarah looked around the crowded service and congratulated herself for choosing the right church. The congregation hummed with little conversations before the service began, and there was a three-year-old group at the nursery available if Annabelle failed to sit still. She smiled to herself when the music began; these people sang in a full-throated gusty bellow that made her feel comfortable singing along. The eleven o'clock service was a nice mix of organ and guitar, so she grinned at the children, found the hymns for them in the back of the missal and sang what she knew. A few families smiled at them despite Robby's seven-year-old fidgeting until he saw a boy and girl he knew from school. Then he straightened and copied their behavior. Leanne simply leaned on Sarah in sleepy mope for most of the service.

When the minister greeted them at the door and welcomed them to the community, Sarah introduced herself shyly. "Good morning. I'm Sarah Monroe. This is Robbie, and then there's Leanne and the sleepy one is Annabelle." Annabelle had wriggled around for the first fifteen minutes and had fallen asleep before communion. Sarah hadn't figured the children would be strangers in the town after living there for two months.

The minister has shaken hands with Robbie and Leanne and said, "Welcome! Monroe? From the farm on the south side of Lilac Hill?" She felt many eyes turned toward them in curiosity as she folded the bulletin carefully and tucked it inside her purse. She nodded and smiled because she'd been the one to paint their family name on the mailbox and nail the whimsical sign to the gatepost four years ago.

After the service, Sarah walked the children through town, surveyed the location of the library, an old-fashioned barber shop, two banks, an ice cream parlor, a large furniture store, grocery and hardware store. At the far end of town, a "Community News" bulletin board advertised local activities like concerts and picnics in a park a short drive away. She jotted a few dates on the church bulletin realizing that Julie's overtaxed worries and her work schedule had kept her from taking the children to these events. Julie's growing depression had kept them home, she corrected in her thoughts.

From visits during her childhood, she knew that the coal mine was another twenty miles away to the south; there was a factory of some sort before the next town and a few diners on the main road. After one day at the farm, she knew that going back to Boston was impossible for the moment. She shivered a little because it was very likely she would visit the diners tomorrow and apply for any daytime work she could get.

At a newsstand outside the grocery, Sarah bought a paper and picked up the free local newspaper with its slim help wanted section. She bought the children ice cream to eat while walking back through town and caught the eye of a group of men getting into their pickups with fishing gear and coolers. Robby ran ahead and waved to one of the men, "How was the fishing, Mr. Stone?"

The man straightened to answer and leaned sideways looking like an old west cowboy to Sarah with his stained jeans, worn plaid shirt over a hole-ridden tee-shirt. He grinned broadly at the little boy, "Just fine, Rob. How are you, boy? Your mama's okay out there on Lilac Hill?" He had glanced up to watch Sarah's approach.

Robby had taken the man's hand in a shake like a gentleman. Sarah was curious at the little boy's mature nature, "I'm fine, and Mama will be just fine now that Aunt Sarah's come home. She's gonna take good care of us, and maybe Mama can be happy again." Robby beamed at the big man.

Sarah stepped forward and extended her hand despite the man's slightly fishy aroma. He took her hand and looked down into her face saying, "Hello, Sarah Monroe. We met at your sister's wedding. I'm Walt Stone." He certainly looked like he'd stepped out of a magazine featuring handsome, rough-cheeked men. Sarah took in his dark bristles meeting long, tapered sideburns and a thin moustache. Not her type of guy at all, but one that might invite all kinds of daydreaming.

Sarah nodded, "Yes, it was three years ago. Thank you for helping Julie. She told me your parents have also been wonderful." He let go of her hand and slid his into his pocket but stared at her intently as she licked her melting ice cream.

Walt Stone seemed to want to say something, but he was drawing a blank. He finally stuttered, "Are you staying for long this time?" The insinuation was that she had been too eager to be away on her other visits.

Sarah shrugged but ran a hand over Leanne's springy hair. The little girl clung to her like a security blanket, "I finished my degree, and it seems Julie needs me for a while." She didn't want to say, "With Michael gone," in front of the children. Walt nodded.

A horn sounded to hurry him to join the caravan of trucks

to some other location. He glanced toward them and waved. "Welcome home, Sarah Monroe. I'm happy you're here, sweetheart." His voice dipped to an odd caressing tenor with the endearment, and he tipped his hat before returning to his truck. Sarah walked on with the children and shook her head at the odd thought of returning home to a place she'd never actually lived in her life. Her parents' roots might be in the area, but Sarah barely remembered trips to visit when she was very young.

Sarah planned to interview for the only job advertised in last week's paper—a morning waitress position at a diner on the main highway near the shoe factory. She was intrigued that there would be a shoe factory in the middle of nowhere, but Julie said the highway and the ability to hire cheap made the place profitable. Julie griped about the mine office in the same way, but often commented on her luck. She thought it was a lucky break to get a bookkeeping job that gave her benefits for three children within a half-hour drive of the farm.

Julie laughed over the thought of church services or the community gatherings. She and Michael had been too busy working in tandem since Annabelle was born to do much socializing. Though the sleepy, little town was closer, she shopped in Wheeling because she could leave the children with friends and get out alone for the day. Julie admitted that she felt embarrassed over Michael leaving without a word and worried over every phone call from the bank, creditors, the police or his family.

If Julie whined at times that she felt old and hemmed in by the demands of the children, Sarah bit her tongue. She avoided pointing out that Julie had been the serial monogamist with the litter of three men in tow, not Sarah. The children were sweet-tempered like their mother, so the resentment that Julie was beginning to build toward them revealed how distressed she had become. The disordered house was another symptom with piles of dirty dishes, mounds of filthy clothes and reams of newspapers and envelopes.

After Sunday services, the clutter and dirt were the first

targets. During that next week, Sarah took a part-time shift at the diner off the highway and called Boston about her delayed return. Sarah gradually cleaned the large house of all the confusion and dirt after working her daily breakfast and lunch shift at the diner.

On the third Sunday since her arrival, Sarah knelt during the communion that she was still too uncomfortable to walk to the altar and receive, as she prayed that some other, better job might surface to help them out. Based on her first real paycheck, the diner job would barely help them though the tips were good. She unfolded the bulletin and glanced over it hoping for business ads to give some direction. Her eye was drawn to a small display advertisement used the name "Lilac Hill" in the logo; it was a notice for applications being taken for an assistant cook, a gardener and two certified childcare workers. She looked closer and saw that it was for the Lambert Research Group at Lilac Hill. She read it two more times in shock. Lilac Hill was her mountain; she hadn't known the wealthy Lambert family lived on the other side of her small mountain.

Thinking about making her application, Sarah skipped the stop for ice cream with the children after church and waved to Walt Stone as they drove by his truck. He was waiting for someone and leaning on the gleaming diesel like he was posed there. Sarah again thought he'd look right at home in a magazine advertisement.

Sarah readied her letter of interest and enclosed an employment history that made her sound like the catch of the century. She even enclosed the evaluation that Chef Jennings had written for her internship. Sarah hoped that they were serious about assistant chef because waiting tables at the diner was draining her spirit. She missed the noisy camaraderie of the staff at Majorane. If she could just begin to cook again, she might regain her equilibrium that was becoming shaky.

Every morning she felt the quivers of the deep worry that raged in her gut as she worked on projects around the farm, managed the children and tried to speak to her sister. If she let a full blown panic attack seize her, she feared she would lose the strength she'd been working on since her father's death four years ago. So Sarah made lists of needed improvements to the farm, the house, the family's diet and habits. She needed to control what she could of the chaos.

CHAPTER 2

Living in Lambertville

"Hey lady! Is that your little girl on the jungle gym? She's stuck at the top and crying!" Sarah snapped out of a light doze when an authoritative voice boomed and a boot nudging her lawn chair broke through a dream. She had been dancing over the rooftops with a handsome man just like Mary Poppins when her eyes opened to register nothing but panic on the empty blanket in front of her.

Where was Annabelle? She shook herself awake and half fell out of the lawn chair only a few hundred feet from the playground as music blared from nearby speakers. Sure enough, her Annabelle was dangling her feet at a large man who was trying to coax her down. His own toddler was squealing at his knees as another man attempted to climb up to Annabelle from the outside of the structure.

Sarah gave the man a half-grunt of thanks and apology but kept the toddler's precarious perch in her sights. She slipped inside the metal structure and awkwardly scaled about six feet above the wood chips until she was below the little girl's feet.

She eased herself next to the child with her next lunge upward and forced a soft, cajoling tone, "Let's go, Annabelle, my love." For a split second, Sarah caught a glimpse of the dramatic sunset that had probably lured the little girl to climb higher like a curious kitten.

Annie stopped crying when faced with the teasing her aunt did to get her to bed. Sarah had learned the little girl reacted to scolding just like her mother; she'd either flee or turn into a turtle. Either reaction would be dangerous ten feet off the ground. The soothing tease worked because the little girl giggled when Sarah added, "Climb down a step there and hold onto me like a little monkey, you imp." Sarah felt every joint in her body tense the moment Annie's hand shifted from its stiff hold on the bar above her. The child carefully climbed next to

Sarah who let go of one hand to position the two year-old into a tight, comfortable grip.

When she was less than three feet off the ground with her joints popping, Sarah said again, "Hang on, my little monkey," crisscrossed her arms around the child and then pulled in her legs to drop with a gentle spring. Her heart was hammering in her chest, and she felt as though she'd aged ten years in the minutes it had taken her to retrieve her niece.

The man with the toddler chuckled at first then stepped forward to admonish Sarah. Annabelle buried her face in Sarah's neck. "You need to keep your eye on that one! She got away too fast." His condescension made the little girl tense immediately and begin to whimper. Sarah heard the appreciative grunts and murmurs of agreement from other adults in the playground area.

Sarah, frazzled from the long work day and the demands of substitute motherhood twelve hours a day, grouched out, "Yes, it would be so much easier if they were all attached to us by little leashes." She gestured from the ridiculousness of his child who would not step away from him to Annabelle who seemed plastered to wild-haired, sweating Sarah.

She swayed a bit in relief, "Sorry, there. I'm exhausted, and I'm still half-asleep." She finally looked up to the irritated man to find the harshly divided features of Jason Lambert frowning down at her. Sarah blanched over being rude to her new employer.

A deep crease grew along the damaged right side of his face as his anger licked red. "I can see that. You were asleep in the chair in less than five minutes." She calmed down from her quick but frightening rescue, and her face reddened. He scolded, "You shouldn't bring them out when you're running on empty." He toned down the scold a bit, but it was still there.

Some other man muttered, "Hey, Mr. Lambert. Give her a break."

Any other time, Sarah could have recovered her humor, but she had spent the entire day in his sticky kitchen with no air conditioning being tested by the taciturn head chef. She'd been treated as if she didn't belong in their fancy kitchen at the mansion. Looking up toward the familiar voice of the other man, Sarah was embarrassed to see Walt Stone and his mother.

She choked back a retort and lost the thought entirely when Annabelle shifted to look up into Sarah's face and ask with a pitiful whine, "Do you really want me on a leash?"

The other people listening laughed, and Sarah regretted her harsh sarcasm with Jason Lambert in the child's presence. She let her voice warm, "No Annabelle, my love. They do not make leashes for little monkeys like you. I do want you stuck to me like glue for the rest of the evening. It's so dark here in the country." She ran a hand down the little girl's back grateful for no broken bones or hysterics.

She turned gracelessly away from the onlookers and scanned the crowd in the fading light, "Let's gather your brother and sister back from friends. I should have brought a flashlight."

As she stepped away she heard Jason Lambert grumble, "Should have stayed in Boston."

That comment broke the spell of embarrassment, and she turned to glare at him. She grumbled back, "I heard that." Her face colored with the blush of knowing he now watched her find and bring the other two children back to their blanket on the grass. He might watch her manage their drink boxes or see the slow droop in her shoulders. Her stomach clenched, and she took slow, deep breaths to find relief.

Exhausted, she finally sat back again and watched the chimney sweeps dance as her five year-old niece copied the steps comically. Her nephew leaned his head on her shoulder and rubbed his face. She finally relaxed into singing all the songs with the crowd after it was truly dark.

Sarah looked about her as the old movie played in a large bowl-shaped park at the base of a valley between a series of hills. The moon was obliterated by clouds, so the stars were also hidden, and the night felt like warm, blue velvet. She gathered the blanket and the basket, her chair and the children well before the end of the movie. She was afraid they all might sob as the beloved nanny packed her bag and left. They stood beside her battered hatchback to see the very end as lightning raced across the looming shadow of a mounded hill to the left. The shape had become familiar in only a few weeks as her mountain, Lilac Hill. Sarah wasn't even surprised when the rain fell in sheets ten minutes after she merged onto the state road on the winding road home from the town community center.

Sarah slept well after the movie except that she dreamed she danced with Jason Lambert over the rooftops, and he scolded her about packing her bags and going home in between fancy steps. After she woke, she replayed scenes of the entire day and only regretted falling into a nap after Robby and Leanne found friends at the park. She wished she could take back her harsh words with Jason Lambert. She'd thought Walt Stone and his parents had been walking toward the park when she pulled into the lot. They had witnessed the embarrassing scene. She knew there was no hope Jason Lambert hadn't recognized her after the comment about Boston.

Looking about her in the darkness of four in the morning, Sarah sighed over the peeling wallpaper and single rectangular window of her small room on Lilac Hill. When she and her sister Julie visited for the first time as adults, Sarah had proudly smoothed a board she found in the old barn, carved the words "Monroe Farm" on the plank for the gate and painted the letters in the pale lavender that she'd painted the front door. Julie said it was ridiculous because a mile from the main road, no one could see the door or the letters, but Sarah had wanted to mark the place theirs in some way. Back in Boston that autumn, she remembered thinking that Lilac Hill was paradise and looked forward to vacationing there a few weeks every year. Four years later, the old farm house was permanently filled with all that was left of her family.

Sarah stretched and turned off the alarm that was set to ring in five minutes. She looked in on Julie. Her sleeping sister had returned home less than an hour ago from the overnight shift at the mine office. It didn't matter that the rest of the world was asleep; at the mine, twenty-four hour operations divided the staff into daytime and night time crews. Even the accounting office operated with a skeleton crew overnight. Julie said that folks had to be paid, contractors came and went all night; and queries and concerns came in from offices all over the globe. Julie liked working through the night. She said it was easier not to worry with the children underfoot all day.

These little slivers of time were the only intersecting moments for the sisters to spend together during the week to balance caring for the children. They communicated through abbreviated lists and the spare half hour between Sarah's return and Julie's run for the truck to drive the thirty miles to work. Sarah felt the weight of this new responsibility even before Jason Lambert caught her napping while Annabelle played daredevil. There was no extra money for daycare, and neighbors had been used as a last resort too many times before she arrived. Sarah had left Boston and a good job to take over childcare for a quick fix.

Sarah's daytime job for Lambert Research would contribute more toward paying off the worst of Julie's debts than waitressing. The unspoken agreement between the sisters assumed that Michael would return in time with some extraordinary excuse for his absence, and Sarah would return to Boston. Neither sister thought this subsistence-level of survival could last very long.

Shared-parenting with Julie was a tightrope walk. Sarah had opinions that she'd squashed for the first few weeks while ferreting out her sister's routines and parenting style. Sometimes Sarah narrowed her eyes to peer caustically at Julie's helter-skelter universe of toys, found objects, laundry piles and messy, poorly-stocked kitchen. The children ate at no prescribed hours and subsisted on cereal, macaroni and cheese, chicken nuggets and hot dogs.

When Sarah took the children into Lambertville for a bit of grocery shopping, she was surprised to discover that they'd never visited the town. It started to sink in after the first few weeks that Julie had been traveling between the farm and her job without venturing out with the children at all. To conserve cash, Sarah didn't wander far from the little town, so by mid-June she and the children became regulars at the grocery, library, church and community gatherings.

When Jason Lambert suggested a return to Boston, he had no idea how good that sounded. Sarah told herself that the town was a quaint break from the city. It was nestled in the picturesque valley encircled by the ancient Blue Ridge Mountains. Her nieces and nephew were genuinely sweet, malleable children, and Monroe Farm was a rough diamond that Sarah knew she could polish up and love. But in Lambertville, Sarah had no promising job at a prestigious restaurant like she'd earned in Boston; she had no collection of co-workers for a pub crawl or a relaxed day shopping. Sarah had no friends here, and the only bar in town was a raucous country dance place.

Sarah had finally wrestled the bills and bank statements from her sister and discovered a stunning, six-figure debt that could take the farm if they defaulted. Julie might spill her worries, but Sarah rarely confided in her sister. Julie didn't seem to hear her when they talked. Sometimes anxiety woke Sarah up and throttled her. Other times, she drove away her tightening gut with breathing exercises and a walk up the mountain path.

On the night of the outdoor movie, when Sarah turned off the state road onto their mile-long drive, she grimaced at the sign she'd put up heralding their name in a spurt of optimism four years ago. There was really no farm at the moment but overgrown, fallow fields. Monroe Farm was a misnomer; Julie hadn't even planted flowers in the porch boxes until Sarah brought them when she arrived in mid-May on the morning she missed commencement. She still had the robe and the fancy velvet cap for a Master's degree recipient hanging in the closet like a ghost from her previous life. And yet, when the sun rose behind the hills across the valley, the golden light on the little farm lit it, and Sarah felt hopeful.

Sarah dressed and packed her little lunch bag with yogurt

and three bottles of water. She expected the thick humidity of Lambert's kitchen with scant air moving through the main part of the house. The dratted Jason Lambert was involved in some experiment with mold that he didn't want sucked up into the ventilation system. One huge fan blew through the kitchen from a far door and made conversation a burden. Sarah wondered what type of scientist he was if he was working with mold.

The sight of her little car blew away grumbling over mold because it was covered nearly to the windows in grass and mud. She smiled grimly to herself as she walked around her little car and squirted it a bit with the garden hose to loosen the worst of the debris. The storm she'd driven into last night had flooded the long driveway to the farmhouse. She was relieved she hadn't blown a tire as they hit bottom a number of times. Once off the main road onto their drive, she thought the car floated a moment before the front tires grabbed. After Annabelle's incident on the playground and the terrible drive home, Sarah felt thankful the children were all in one piece and sleeping soundly in the house.

During the bumpy drive out to the main road and around the mountain to the Lambert's mansion, Sarah decided to apologize with sincerity if necessary, bite her acerbic tongue, and focus on learning the head chef's routines, as she'd done with Chef David in Boston. Margaret Turner was a thin, older woman with an iron back and an unfriendly demeanor. Sarah had been relieved to see Maggie's reserve crack for a moment when the stern woman tried Sarah's raw dough for the tarts she made yesterday. Trained by a pastry maestro in her Boston restaurant, Sarah understood the delicate balance that must not be disrupted when a cooking assistant was added to the staff. She had blundered and done herself out of a job during her first internship in Boston by chatting too much and making suggestions. Humility and silence were generally rewarded. Sarah sometimes thought she might earn a doctorate in those two virtues.

Sarah slipped into the kitchen at 4:30 a.m. and put a pot of coffee on to brew like she noticed Margaret made. She tied on her apron and read the entire menu posted on the board. Her initials were next to the assignments she had agreed to yesterday. At the bottom was a bit of a note, "J. Lambert raved over blueberry tarts. Try another berry tart today." The "J" could be Joseph who was the silver-haired and flirty head of the household or Jason who was the ultimate grouch and king of mold. Sarah grimaced and began those first because Mr. Jason Lambert was the first to come down to breakfast yesterday, and she expected that he followed that pattern daily.

By the time Margaret tied her apron on, the tarts were finished and ready for service, juice was assembled and Sarah was humming through a quick bread with leftover zucchini from the evening meal. She was removing the toasted walnuts from the oven when Margaret nodded and said, "Good morning, Sarah."

Sarah smiled and uttered a matching, "Good morning, Miss Turner," as Jason Lambert came into the room for his coffee. He was completely dressed at six a.m. in dress pants, shirt and tie and waved a mug at Margaret though she glared at him. No one was allowed in Margaret's kitchen first thing in the morning, even the boss. "You didn't order early coffee, Mr. Jason!" She poured him one anyway. He raised an eyebrow, as Sarah's eyes fell, and she moved away to toss the walnuts into the mix.

She stirred it delicately once and then poured the batter into the tins. Popping the ten miniature loaves into the oven, she ignored their conversation about a fancy dinner service planned for the following week. Sarah turned to the bread dough that she had left to rise for the last thirty minutes and began to cut and form the loaves.

When he spoke, Sarah jumped because he was nearly at her ear, "I suppose you managed to get all those poor children home in the deluge?" His voice lowered to scold. "You should have left the community center earlier." She feared he wanted to goad her to snap at him again.

Resisting, she nodded and then turned her face sideways to look at him boldly, "I apologize for my rudeness last night,

Mr. Lambert. Thank you for looking out for Annabelle." Near the long scar on his cheek, a nerve twitched. Her eyes fell to his hands that clenched the mug too tight. He was angry for some reason.

"Someone ought to look out for you. Your car looks like you took it off-road last night on the way home. And your tires are bald. What are you thinking by driving all over the valley with three little children like that? I wasn't kidding about returning to Boston, Miss Monroe." They both looked at the mess in her hands; Sarah had unconsciously kneaded one of the little loaves into an oozy blob that would never rise. He looked at it on the counter and frowned. He turned and began to leave. Sarah turned to gape at him.

Behind his back, Maggie stared at them with a gaping mouth. His voice snapped Sarah's eyes back to his frown, "One of the yardmen is washing your car. It's on its last legs, you know." He looked surprised that she wasn't angry, just tearful. He had said aloud exactly what she had been thinking that morning.

Sarah lowered her eyes and said, "Thank you, sir." There was nothing more to say that would patch it up, so Sarah tossed the ruined loaf in the trash, spread a few handfuls of sesame seed on a tray and popped that in the oven for scarce moments. She decided that the Lamberts should introduce sesame seed bread into their plain bread diet. She gave a wan smile to Margaret Turner and began the next dish.

Sarah spent that week encased in a silence so thick she was able to ignore Jason Lambert's intrusion into the hurry of the morning kitchen whether he was dressed in a suit or stumbling around after an all-night work session in his shorts. She was puzzling out the likes and dislikes of every person in the household, counting the staff in idle concentration, and watching Margaret Turner hone the food order with precision. She liked working on Miss Maggie's light ship far better than the unwieldy craft in Boston run by the often silly, rather verbose Chef Jennings. The older woman contrasted sharply with the screaming-maniac chef and owner of Majorane. Chef David had been intuitive and dramatic; Margaret Turner was versatile but taciturn.

Sarah had realized quickly during her Boston training that calm detachment was the best defense with dictators, and she used what she'd learned on Jason Lambert. She created a cushy pillow that shielded her when he brushed by her in the hall or glared at her every morning. He asked about the children often. *How old was Robby? How old?* That second question was asked with a sneer and a bold look at her figure that puzzled her. *Did Leanne have the same color hair as her father?* His eyes glittered over her raven-brown hair pulled tight at her nape and off her face. *Had she kept an eye on Annabelle carefully enough at the library the other day? What kind of name was "Annabelle" anyway?*

Most of these questions, she answered monosyllabically and forced quick-witted sarcasm to the back of her throat. In her mind and sometimes later to Maggie's more subtle probing, she gave brief but lyrical answers that revealed how much she'd come to understand Julie's children. Robby was seven now, getting tall and threatening to become as handsome as his doe-eyed father who was killed in Iraq. Leanne's daddy was a devil, yes, with a luscious head of reddish-brown hair like the Irishman she thought he was. And no, she obviously had not kept track of Annabelle, her little imp, in the library because everyone in the county heard the shelf of movies crash to the floor. Sarah had been distracted with coaching Leanne through a storybook page she was attempting to sound out. And the name "Annabelle" was bestowed in honor of her sister's best friend from Trenton who had died of cancer the month the baby was born. Annabelle from Trenton had been twenty-seven and dear, dear, dear.

Large tears rolled down for that one, and Maggie patted Sarah on the back. That afternoon, they rolled dough for twenty pies that were mixed with memories. The pies caused such a bidding contention at the church auction that Maggie Turner and Isabel Lambert pledged double the number for the next sale.

Jason Lambert listened to her speak from the hallway and wondered what to make of Sarah Monroe.

CHAPTER 3

Revelations of Gravel

It wasn't the actual gravel order, her gutsy independence over fixing the driveway, the use of the children to fetch buckets with gardening trowels, or even the wreck she made of her hands that inspired his ire over the repair of the road to the Lilac Hill farm. It was the unabashed report given by her eldest child, that brave little voice of Robert Reilly in the hardware, explaining their parentage without reserve or notice of the shock on people's faces that worked up new irritation with Sarah. Jason Lambert strode away from her bunch of wildflowers called children and wished he never asked the question and exposed them to public ridicule.

He'd noticed her walking them into the grocery store earlier with a short list as she conversed merrily with the reddish-haired one who sat inside the cart while the little one who looked so much like Sarah was strapped loosely in the top child seat. Little Robby walked beside his collection of females with the gape of most out-numbered men in the world. He just blinked and listened to their chatter as they sailed around the store selecting this and that. She chose to buy very little that morning, stowed it in the car and hurried all three children across the busy main street against the light. Sarah had that look of a woman on a mission.

Beside him in the barber's chair, his father said, "Is that our pastry chef with her famous collection of children? They do look like nice, little children," his father winked at Jason because his son had complained bitterly about her lack of parenting skills and her careless driving willy-nilly all over the valley with them. His father had been reading the paper when their main cook Margaret had come in and cautioned Jason to stay out of the kitchen if he was going to pick fights with the best pastry chef they had ever lured to the house. He had said something to Sarah that morning that had aroused such distress that the meringues wouldn't rise on the half dozen lemon pies ordered for Miss Isabel's luncheon. He simply had to stay out of the kitchen and to please leave Sarah alone.

A third man in the barbershop sat forward and grinned, "The youngest child is a friend of mine's little girl. Very sweet and precocious just like her mama," the large man cocked an eyebrow at Jason who glanced back at Sarah disappearing into the town hardware store. Jason Lambert wondered what she was up to out at the farm and crossed the street as soon as his haircut was finished.

Sarah puzzled Jason to the extreme. Nothing on her work application had mentioned children; she hadn't asked about a family healthcare plan; she hadn't checked "married," but few people checked that area anymore. If he hadn't seen her at the community center last month watching an outdoor movie, he might not even know the children existed based on her scant personal talk in the kitchen. Jason Lambert's irritation with Sarah twisted into an odd attraction from that initial argument at the jungle gym, and it grew despite her deep, stoical quiet which seemed to have no bottom.

At the counter in the back of the hardware store, he overhead her ask about a load of gravel when Eddie, the oldest son of the hardware store owner, finally decided to wait on her. The boy probably couldn't imagine that a woman would make a serious purchase with three little children winding about her like kittens. Distracted by a bin of tape measures, the oldest, a boy with dark-hair and round, brown eyes was probably tall for seven. The little girl who bounced along and stretched away from her brother's grasp had the reddish-brown curls, green eyes and dimples of a Scotsman. The youngest girl nestled against Sarah's thigh had the exact deep brown hair as Sarah and eyes a slightly lighter blue. He knew the littlest one—Annabelle--was caught at that mischievous stage between two and three-years-old. Jason's own little girl Chloe had passed that stage just a few months ago. Jason looked at Sarah's unaffected, low-slung jeans and a tee-shirt with a band logo and could easily imagine her on a university campus but not a mother to these three.

He stepped forward as she asked about the different grades of gravel and could not answer the clerk's question about what they had down. Jason was about to speak up because he had ordered that gravel himself a few years back before the place went on the market. Sarah's little boy stepped forward in excitement. Robby grinned and emptied his pants pocket on the counter, "Here they are—well a couple of them that looked like good skippers. May I have them back later?" Jason smiled when Sarah laughed. Jason held out a hand to the five-year-old and asked the seven-year-old a question about some nails the boy was holding to give her time to think.

Sarah finished her order and paid for the delivery from a tight roll of cash pulled out of her front pocket. Another child who'd come into the store with his parents yelled to the boy, "Hey, Reilly!" and had made Jason curious. He asked Robby why the boy called him "Reilly," and the little boy gave a speech in a practiced rendition, "My Dad's name was Robert Allan Reilly, but I'm Robert John for my granddad. Now Leanne, here, her last name is Thompson for her daddy, but we divorced him. He was mean." The child gestured toward little Annabelle who giggled and hid her face on Sarah's leg again as Sarah whirled around aghast at this public announcement of their parentage. "You've met Annabelle, she is an Elliott, and her father Michael is very nice, but he hasn't been back in a while." Jason's heart lurched, as the little boy's face fell in sorrow, and the girls nodded in agreement. Sarah's eyes flew around the store to see who else was listening. Eddie was frozen with his mouth wide open in the act of handing Sarah the receipt. Her face and neck mottled with a blush, and everything about her sharpened into angles.

Jason tried to brush over it, "Well, thanks for explaining it so clearly, Robby. Most adults wouldn't know how to explain it so well."

Robby nodded as Sarah got her receipt and jammed it into her other pocket. There were tears beginning in her eyes that might fall on the way back out to the house. Robby agreed solemnly, "Mom says most adults make family too complicated." Jason nodded seriously and met Sarah's eye as the blush flamed scarlet through her cheeks, neck and chest.

On Monday morning when he took her to task about using the children for the labor of spreading a whole ton of gravel, he was horrified that she had collected these children like fruit from a produce department of men. She was confused by his insistence that she was a terrible influence and a careless provider. Sarah only admitted on a sigh, "I am doing the best that I can."

He exploded at that and said, "It will be a horror at school, Sarah! They have three different last names?"

She had been preparing pie crust when he started his morning editorial on the role of Sarah in the lives of the Monroe children. As he spoke, she crushed the dough to pebbles and then stilled her hands on the pastry stone locking her wrists and fingers in tension. The pastry stone was set in the counter before a large casement window. Sarah squinted at her view of the pastures and the back of the great barn. She did not understand why this man was so angry over her management of her sister's children.

Her mouth angled into a deep frown, and she narrowed her eyes slowly until everything was black and white outlines. She noticed that he had stopped speaking, though she couldn't remember what his last chiding question might have been. Her voice was roughened from distress but pleaded, "It is fine to be concerned, sir, but unless you have some sensible solution, please don't talk to me about the children or their welfare again. Every time you speak to me, the dough I'm making fails. Please leave me alone, so I can do my job. Fire me if I annoy you so much."

He laughed out loud over her quiet, eloquent protest. He watched as she threw out her entire first batch of dough and wiped the counters, waiting until he left the room to begin again.

CHAPTER 4

Isabel's Questions

"How is the new hire? That pastry chef from Boston?" After three weeks of the best berry tarts she'd ever eaten, Isabel Lambert had asked to see Margaret Turner about Sarah Monroe. Margaret, a spry sixty-five year-old, examined alarming changes in the younger Isabel. Margaret worried over the accelerated aging in this woman whom she'd thought of as a friend for over forty years. When Joseph Lambert had returned from college engaged to twenty-one-year-old Isabel, Margaret was working in the Lambert kitchen under their aged head cook.

Maggie smiled thinking about Sarah repeating Maggie's role in the household. "Talented. Quiet, but efficient. Dependable." Maggie arched a brow at Isabel's interest. Old Billy Painter had been working for them for ten years, but Isabel never asked about his heavy muffins or thick gravies.

Maggie glanced at Isabel's silk blouse and lounge pants, but she did not let her eyes stray and examine her own habitual cotton pants and kitchen smock. By twenty-six, Margaret had been married for six years and had learned to balance two children with the demands of the job. Her husband was in Korea, and his family pitched in to mind the boys while she worked. Isabel had admired Margaret's fighting spirit and her independence. They met for the first time to trade more creative recipes for a dinner party. Even after Joseph and Isabel moved to New York to build his law practice, Maggie and Isabel continued to trade letters filled with clippings, observations and stories from their otherwise, dissimilar lives.

Isabel smiled, "I didn't quite believe everything on her application. Joseph had just put the ad in the church bulletin. She called and inquired while he was away, so I hired her." She looked troubled. "I didn't connect her last name to Lilac Hill until Joseph returned from his trip to New York." Maggie noticed Isabel's fingers trembling.

Moving back from New York to help raise her youngest grandchild had been detrimental to Isabel, who loved living in the city far from her husband's roots. Isabel had thrived on the hubbub of New York City where she'd spent the last thirty years. Her children were much more tied to the old Lambert property than she was. Nearly four years ago, her eldest son Jason exercised his birthright to live in the monstrous house that he had since retrofitted, accommodating his returning parents and a research lab that employed a staff of twenty-five. His younger brother Stephen lived outside Pittsburgh with his wife and two children, but they were regular weekend guests.

"I wouldn't worry over the Monroe name—Sarah is a good fit in the kitchen. I've let her create a few of the entrees with Billy as her assistant. They make a good team." She thought about the ease she noticed between the young woman and the older man who was usually brusque and argumentative.

Isabel nodded, "You manage them well. Not many people would want to take on Billy Painter and his opinionated tongue. You've mastered him!" Isabel laughed, "I think you like all the mess of the lab staff and our busy family."

Margaret smirked, but she agreed, "I like the added activity of the research lab. And I enjoy creating menus with your Jason. He is a good man." She had enjoyed both of their children for the brief time the Lamberts had lived at the mansion when he was younger, but she admired Jason as a man. Maimed in the accident that killed his wife, he had retreated to heal. He had reinvented his father's inheritance as laboratory that did sub-contracting business with old government contacts and serviced some entreaties from private industry. The year Joseph retired from his law practice in New York, Jason's wife had been killed in the accident that injured him gravely. After Jason was released from the hospital, his parents packed their apartment and came home to Lambertville in central West Virginia.

Isabel often said that family did that for each other, but she yearned for their hectic social life in the city, fine meals in fancy restaurants and cultural events. When Isabel Lambert said she hired the last cook based on the fact that she was an accomplished pastry chef, Margaret was rueful but hardly surprised. Infusing new blood and fancy ideas into their commonplace meals might enliven them. With that impulse, Sarah Monroe had been added to the eclectic kitchen staff.

Margaret found the new pastry chef an interesting girl. She had large, expressive eyes and a dancer's body under the tightly-fastened apron. Tall and dark-haired with a face that fell to a pensive, pouting expression, Margaret couldn't read her new assistant. The girl sniffed at the odor of moss and mold on the first day when the air conditioning was turned off, but she sweated in silence. She asked a minimum of questions and observed Margaret with uncomfortable concentration. Margaret understood that the girl was matching her habits to the head chef's expectations.

Freed to interpret the menu items independently, Sarah's creations were inspired but flawlessly simple. She appeared to create silky fillings and layers of delicate dough by pressure alone using the same ingredients they had always purchased. She required no fancy machines or implements as Margaret first feared. She pitched in for the main dishes and revealed a sense of taste and a rhythm of work that was astounding for an inexperienced cook.

After only two days, Maggie Turner had concluded that, beyond excellent pastry and silent obedience, the girlish woman was a fine creature. Sarah held her counsel when faced with unfairness and bit her tongue on ready comments Maggie saw in the tightening of her muscles in her back. Maggie thought Sarah Monroe contained a gentle humor that was infectious. She was not afraid to laugh at her own shortcomings. She was not proud or self-involved.

Isabel was curious, "So why is Jason so interested in her? I have never eaten pastries so fine, and it would be a shame to lose her. And did you have her make the lasagna yesterday? I knew it wasn't yours— I still prefer yours, but the recipe was intriguing!" Isabel had also spied Jason's hurry as the pastry chef took a turn in the garden on her break. He'd met her in the center trying to seem casual, but his mother had smiled to see them speak with some intensity and watched as he caught her hand and looked as though he dared to kiss it.

Margaret sat beside Isabel and smiled. "You hired her. I don't know how it happened that she moved here, but she's very good. After I reviewed her resume and told her the hours and pay, I thought she'd rather interview at a Wheeling restaurant for a more prestigious position. You know, she doesn't just have a degree from a small culinary school. There's also a Master's degree from a university." Maggie did not tell Isabel about the three little children or the tension she'd noticed that plagued their new chef.

Isabel digested this information and thought about her son's brush of a kiss on the young woman's hand that day. Jason was enamored with this Sarah. Her heart ached when she thought of her son trying to attract a girl as young as this one. At thirty-eight, Jason lived the life of a much older man. Sometimes her son seemed older than either of his parents.

Isabel leaned closer to Margaret to whisper, "Maggie, I think Jason likes her. This would be the first time he was interested in a woman since Annette died. What is she really like?" The thought of his ravaged features and the healed sutures that she'd tended herself made her shrink. The girl she'd spied seemed too fine to settle for such a man unless she could see beyond the surface. The young woman would be stonewalled by his gruff seriousness unless she could delve beneath the hard attitude. He'd put on the tough outer layer long before the accident when his marriage had soured.

Maggie nodded, "I don't know much about her, but she is quiet and efficient. She doesn't startle easily and takes constructive criticism well. Except for Jason, she has gotten along well with everyone here." Maggie's eyes danced at sliding that one into the conversation.

"She doesn't get along with Jason? I saw them in the garden this morning, and I thought he was kissing her hand!" Isabel's interest was now completely engaged. She had color in her cheeks, and her breath was rapid with the mystery of it.

Maggie nodded and told it like a wonderful secret, "Oh, yes. Jason yelled at her for spreading gravel out at her place. Seems she had a load of gravel delivered last weekend and skimped on having it spread for her. He happened by there as she and her family finished the job. This morning, I gave her some ointment for the blisters, and Jason caught us."

She swallowed; this part must be handled better in the future because she knew the girl had been insulted by him, "He comes into the kitchen nearly every morning now for his coffee." She crooked her eyebrow high, "He might not intend it, but he often says the rudest things. He's probably trying to get a rise out of her. She just ducks her head like a turtle and takes it. She's only spoken back to him a couple of times and seems puzzled by his attention. I think she's convinced that he wants her to quit." With that said, Maggie stood beside Isabel and placed a hand on the other woman's shoulder. "I don't care how old they are, we never stop being their mothers, do we?"

Isabel laughed as she caught onto Maggie's intention. "Yes, I guess he needs his mother just as much as he did when he was little. Thank you, Maggie, you are a good friend."

While the rest of the staff finished their one o'clock break before preparation for the evening meal began, Sarah wandered the gardens and stretched. It was usually very hot, so no one joined her or interrupted her meditation. These moments of quiet reflection were just as important as rising on time each day, eating her regimental yogurt, drinking three bottles of water and reading from her favorite collection of essays. Sarah had developed these habits to battle the worries that turned into panic that had raged through her since her father's death. It wasn't just his passing that hurt so much; it was the chaos that befell the two Monroe sisters since his heart attack that shoveled on the intermittent pain. When their mother had been diagnosed with cancer, there had been a little time for reckoning with the disease, the threat of her death and then her painful end. With their father, no time for preparations had occurred. He was healthy one moment and gone in the next of a massive heart attack. His death had ripped open any healing from their mother's loss and tossed them into deeper grief.

John Monroe had been Sarah's rock; the big man had supported and guided her more than she'd understood until after his steady presence was missing. She had watched her sister cartwheel into odd decisions, burn bridges and start over after they settled the estate. Sarah had battled depression after their house in Trenton sold, but she forced herself to return to school and the rigorous schedule. She missed the normalcy of school. She missed her father's gentle guidance and support.

The panic attacks started after Julie's impulsive wedding day less than six months after their father's funeral. She had hyperventilated on the bus trip home to Boston and had missed a week of classes and work plagued by anxiety. One of her friends had visited and diagnosed it immediately. The round of doctors' visits had educated Sarah in a new vocabulary she called "depression-speak." Sarah had recovered from years of episodic panic attacks that once froze her, but she understood the fragility of her control. The heat in the garden was nothing in the face of regaining peace and balance in her brain. Sometimes if she felt on the verge of dark thoughts at the Lambert Mansion, she began running full speed as she cleared the back garden gate. The one o'clock break was the only time she was alone in this new life after spending most of her time quietly healing during the solitary years in Boston.

Sarah walked back with heaving lungs after a long run the day Jason Lambert touched her hands. His words were harsh and demeaning as ever, she expected that from him, but his touch had been gentle, and his lips had nearly grazed her palm as he inspected the blisters. She twitched her sore back muscles from the gravel spreading on the weekend. It felt good to hurt from real work. Other people might find the tension of standing while kneading, rolling and stretching all day a workout, but Sarah craved heavy, physical activity. She wanted to deaden the twitching muscles at night when she reviewed every conversation from her day and rewound any featuring him. She rolled her shoulders like a prize fighter when she thought of Jason Lambert. He irritated her; he insulted her; she was attracted to him. It was galling.

Sarah nearly growled at the thought of her employer as her object of attraction. He was startlingly ugly with the aftereffects of the terrible accident marking his face, neck and even his arms when he exposed them. He was a hulking thing, probably six-three and large-boned with it. With his towering frame, she expected him to be clumsy. Instead he was quick and agile, nearly silent on his feet as he slipped into the kitchen and watched her work, or smooth as he blocked her escape on a few occasions.

Earlier he had met her on the garden path and had taken her hands to run a light finger over her blistered palms. The thrill had swept her whole body, and she knew he'd noticed because his blue irises had all but disappeared as their eyes met. He'd made her feel weak, but he'd wrecked it by cautioning, "You shouldn't use the children for work like that." Her cheeks had rushed scarlet as she pulled away from him. The children had enjoyed getting outside and examining the gray rocks, hauling miniature buckets to each pothole and dumping them. In her mind's eye, she saw every windowsill in each of their rooms decorated with choice stones she let each of them choose to keep as prizes for their day of labor.

Her words back to him had been ill-chosen in irritation, "Work? It was a game to them. They need to understand that the ruts needed to be filled to make it safer for us when it rains. They were outside with me and not making messes in the house." She had wanted to stop, but the words poured out. "The children need to understand where the money goes that we don't spend on the latest toy. Certainly, they are not spoiled brats, but they have never been abused as child laborers." She hadn't meant that his little girl was spoiled, but he heard it that way. His pupils shrunk to pin dots in that moment, and he squeezed her hands painfully. She'd pulled her hands away and had hurried back into the kitchen to finish her shift. Her heart pounded as she remembered the anger in his face, so she waited to be fired all the rest of that day.

When Isabel Lambert appeared in the garden the day after that poorly-executed conversation, Sarah Monroe expected to hang up her apron and go back to work at the diner outside of town. She had never in her life let a man slip under her skin before, and it was uncomfortable. Having Maggie Turner, Lou and Billy there and observing it added to the tension.

Isabel looked proper with her powdered makeup, pale-blue lounging outfit and perfectly-coifed, gray waves, but her manner was warm, "Miss Sarah, come over here a moment! I hoped you would walk this way today!" Suddenly Sarah realized that she might be intruding on a private garden in her walks and made a mental note to ask Maggie if servants were permitted to walk the gardens. "Come see these butterflies. They were the ugliest caterpillars I'd ever seen, right Chloe?" The little girl emerged from beneath the shadow of Isabel's flowing sleeves and nodded seriously.

Chloe worked up the courage to speak as Sarah nodded and leaned toward the bush filled with blossoms and beautiful yellow moths with blue dots circled in black like eyes ringed with mascara for a wild night on the town. Sarah smiled as one flitted close to Isabel's outstretched hand. The little girl's voice was hushed in awe of the moths and Sarah's new person, "I told Grandma not to be afraid of them. They're moths. We can look them up in here." Chloe tapped the little book she clasped in her other hand. Sarah glanced at the very adult guide to insects of the Eastern United States and grinned. The little girl might be a scientist like her father.

The girl started to flip through the guide and found the appropriate page. She opened it wider for her grandmother and Sarah to see the likeness of the giant moth and its very ugly version as a caterpillar. Sarah nodded, "Thank you, Chloe. I understand that butterflies and bees are very important to gardens."

Chloe nodded, "Without them some plants would die out. Pollination is done by bees and butterflies." Sarah gasped at the little girl's vocabulary. Though she thought Chloe was nearly four, she spoke like a miniature adult.

Isabel nodded at Sarah's open face, "And the transformation from ugly caterpillar which eats the garden to beautiful butterfly or moth which pollinates the garden is a necessary cycle. Painful but necessary."

Sarah tilted her head at the pair, "I have never considered the pain of the chrysalis. I always thought it was like death and rebirth." She blinked as the woman and child smiled at each other.

Isabel laughed gently, "I knew there was a poet behind all those flaky layers of pastry at breakfast. Chloe and I would like to ask a favor. I am a fine natural science tutor for Chloe, but she is curious about baking. Seems her father enjoys your version of sweets, and Chloe would like to try her hand. Something simple will do." Isabel's eyes flashed a pleading look at Sarah that melted away immediately. Their gazes caught, and then Isabel's eyes fell into looking into a middle distance of memory.

Sarah narrowed her eyes because an entirely different conversation seemed to have occurred in the undercurrents. Ugly caterpillars and beautiful moths? She nodded and spoke directly to Chloe, "I will order ingredients for pastry you want to learn. Is there any recipe in particular you want to try?"

Chloe smiled and was suddenly a child again, "Cookies! Chocolate chip or oatmeal."

Sarah nodded. She was relieved that Chloe hadn't asked for the tarts that frustrated Maggie. The woman was frustrated with learning not to over mix before rolling and then taking a gentle hand to the dough. The orders for fruit tarts increased by the day. "I've never made cookies here. It will be fun. Today or tomorrow? We have all the ingredients for cookies on hand." She looked back to Isabel Lambert who was still distracted. The woman startled and looked back at Sarah with narrowed eyes and pursed lips.

Chloe pressed her lips together and thought for a moment, "Painting lessons are today. Tomorrow after breakfast? Daddy says I am not to take too much of your time." The little girl's hair was nearly white in the bright sun, and her skin glowed pale peach.

Before they parted, Isabel abruptly asked, "What is your full name again, Miss Sarah? I just realized I barely paid attention the day you interviewed."

The little girl chortled out a laugh, "Grandma! This is Sarah Monroe. Daddy has told you!"

Isabel stood up straight and croaked out, "From Monroe Farm on the other side of Lilac Hill?" At Sarah's nod, Isabel whispered because the question choked her, "How are your parents, Sarah Monroe?"

Blinking either from the sun in her eyes or the sorrow the words might unleash, Sarah stated, "Both have died. My mother—six years ago and Daddy—four."

Isabel's mouth slanted over time that passed without notice. She came to accounts with the news of the deaths of loved and hated ones. Isabel uttered, "I am sorry that you lost them, Sarah. Mr. Lambert thought he was selling the farm to your father, you know. He wondered why your parents never came back after the sale was final."

Sarah nodded and hurried back to the kitchen to begin the afternoon preparations. She put aside the quiet sorrow that clenched her heart when she thought of her protective parents who were absent but somehow more present on Lilac Hill.

She relaxed over planning the lesson with Chloe because Jason Lambert knew Miss Isabel's plan. He seemed to find fault with her parenting skills but approved of her baking. Encouraging lessons with Chloe insinuated she could handle children on some level. She smiled at her own distracted thoughts.

That night she pulled down her mother's cookbooks from the cabinet above the dishes they'd used growing up. She and the three children tried both recipes until late and giggled over tummies full of cookie dough. The house filled with the smell of warm chocolate and oatmeal with raisins. When Julie returned at three in the morning, she looked in on Sarah who stirred half-awake to accept the brush of a kiss on her cheek.

Julie whispered, "I love it when you bake, little sister." Sarah smiled and fell into a deep sleep that was hard to shake an hour later.

Chloe's baking lessons extended into cooking lessons from Maggie and Lou, the afternoon chef. Lou and Maggie might have directed the hints and tips to Chloe, but Sarah realized immediately that they were designed to include her and draw her out of a self-imposed silence. Chloe laughed infectiously as she chopped carrots, diced tomatoes correctly and learned to handle onions without turning into a runny-nosed, teary-eyed wreck. Sarah watched Lou and Maggie play off of each other's strengths as they prepared a rich menu for the family and staff. She understood that this working relationship was just as important as the knowledge of food, its myriad combinations and preparations.

CHAPTER 5

Dinner Parties and Tires

In order to host a big dinner party in Lambertville, daycare had to be provided for employees. The evening was usually planned to end earlier than in the city because the commutes were ferocious. The food, though, was to be on par with a five-star restaurant. Preparation could go on for days, but this one crept up on the Lamberts due to the research staff's tension over the newest government contract. Isabel Lambert actually visited the kitchen and lured the entire staff into the dining room to organize a reception for visiting government officials and the laboratory staff. Jason rushed through and rolled his eyes but promised overtime for the extra hours in deference to his mother's mania over parties. He had arranged for a simple roast beef dinner with fruit tarts for dessert. Isabel had invited the mayor and then the sheriff which led to a list that grew slowly to dinner for fifty.

Sarah worried over bringing the children to the Lambert house. Leanne had developed a fascination with Jason and asked a zillion questions about his scars that Sarah tried to discourage. When they saw Jason and his little daughter Chloe in the library or at community center activities, Leanne made a mad dash to smile in her simpering version of little girl flirting. Annabelle would normally wave to Chloe who was seldom friendly just like her father. An evening earning double-time pay was tempting, but Sarah begged off because of the children. She confided to Maggie, "Jason Lambert is too scandalized by them." She did not want to bring the children to the mansion and expose herself to more of his opinions.

In the desire to impress, Isabel had hired a chef from a well-known restaurant in Wheeling to make a few signature dishes. A tall, overly muscular man, Michel de Gault arrived with a bluster of demands as the gardeners helped to bring his cartons of ingredients into the kitchen. Sarah watched the man preen like a peacock but hid her smirk at the man's affectations. She cocked an eyebrow at Lou and Billy, the afternoon team, as the buffoon insulted Margaret Turner. The hired chef tasted Maggie's marinade for lamb and said it was old-fashioned but palatable though no one had invited his opinion. He tried to filch more than one of Sarah's miniature tarts, but she moved them away from his fingertips. He inspected the kitchen noisily using an affected French accent that wobbled into downtown Atlanta as his irritation grew. Sarah grinned to herself, kept her own counsel and looked forward to leaving at four before the man blew up for the first time. Chefs like Michel de Gault played their parts with high theatrics.

When the ingredients for his dishes were assembled at the largest work station, he waved away Sarah's assistance. She shrugged and fled to help Billy with the side dishes. She remained stoic over Michel's criticism that the assistant chef was no more than a schoolgirl. "Pastry and chef should never be said in the same breath," he'd intoned expecting her ire. Sarah rolled her eyes at the outlandish statement and grumbled, "I was good enough to work with Chef Jennings at Majorane in Boston." Michel rolled his eyes back and dismissed her with a wave of the hand.

Sarah's canapés, desserts, dinner rolls and breads had been finished hours before in a flurry of mixing, pounding, cutting and baking, so she cleaned the work stations, checked the plating preparations for service and prepared to leave for the day. At a spate of curses from Michel, Sarah and Billy watched in amused horror as the fancy chef self-destructed.

As he had begun to assemble his dishes, he fumbled a sauce, burned a pan of onions and mushrooms into glop and found the cheese he needed hadn't been grated to his liking. When the infuriated man began to curse and stomp over the temperature of the butter, Sarah sniggered and looked at Billy. Michel burst into flame over having the wrong type of virgin olive oil. Billy grumbled, "I'm going out back to smoke a cigarette." By the time the man let another stream of curses explode over something minor, Jason Lambert walked in for his afternoon duel with Sarah.

That evening Jason strode over to Chef Michel de Gault with his hands resting on his hips. Michel's slack jaw and widened eyes examined Jason's irritation and exposed scars. Jason had heard the idiotic stream of nonsense from the hallway, and he ordered the chef, "Sortez de chez moi, tyran."

Michel looked at Jason blankly and asked, "What?"

Maggie Turner spoke up from the browning, succulent lamb she was basting with her "old-fashioned" marinade. "He said 'scram' you charlatan!" And then she grinned to make it all the better. The great man packed up his tools and left the building quickly.

Maggie shrugged, "Sarah, take over his dishes. I know you can make something with all those fancy ingredients that Miss Isabel wanted. Sarah needs someone to go and fetch the children if the meal is to be ready on time." She eyed both Sarah and Jason who gazed at her in shock. Billy returned to the kitchen grinning at the stream of curses he heard Michel expel as his car kicked up gravel in the drive.

Billy chuckled and raised his hand, "I'll go fetch them. Thanks for giving that fool his walking orders, Mr. Lambert!"

Sarah shook her head, "Mr. Lambert doesn't want the children here. Maggie, I'll get the courses readied by five and the three of you can finish. I'll call my sister and see if she can leave for work a bit later than usual."

Jason blinked at her, "Sarah! How can you think that? If you can recover from the mess that pompous jerk left, I'll pay all four of you what my mother promised him as a bonus. Good enough?" Sarah agreed as the other three silently begged her.

After she called home and urged Julie to caution each of the children to be on their best behavior, Sarah found herself in the hallway alone with Jason Lambert as he jangled car keys. He gravely extended a hand for her to shake. When she looked up to ask what they were shaking on, he said quietly, "I'll drive over to your place for them. And we need to call a truce, Sarah. I do not dislike or seek to avoid your children. I think they're charming, all considered." His eyes seemed friendlier for once, and his physical nearness pricked up the hairs on her arms.

Sarah nodded and added very quietly but sharply, "All considered me and the fact that I should go home to Boston. Yes, Mr. Lambert, I understand your general opinion." She turned abruptly and left him staring after her.

Sarah walked back into the kitchen, examined the remaining ingredients, tossed out the general tone of Michel's recipes, reviewed the rest of the menu and assembled three dishes far better than de Gault was capable. Lou, Pete and Maggie watched Sarah's slight grin as she hummed and worked on three dishes simultaneously. As she gave orders, they winked at each other. In her element, Sarah was her own version of a dictator, but she was a quietly civil one.

When she collected the children later, she found them in the company of Chloe, Jason and his brother Stephen. Jason introduced Sarah to his brother, "This is our incredible pastry chef." She smiled at the seldom praise from Jason. Jason's brother was younger, even-featured and openly friendly. Sarah blushed remembering him from the night of the community center movie and the episode with Annabelle.

The Monroe children picked up their belongings and thanked Jason without prodding. On the way to the car, Isabel rushed back through the house and pulled Sarah back into the dining room to meet the dignitaries and the owner of a new restaurant in Wheeling. The story of Sarah saving the three dishes abandoned by Michel de Gault had been raved over by Maggie when she visited the tables as head chef. Sarah blushed and thanked them for the praise.

Sarah's face blanched when Robby spoke up with regally childish authority, "You're lucky; she usually makes us eat vegetables and healthy stuff like that!" He grinned as Jason snuck a small bag of desserts into Leanne's grasp. Sarah hushed all of them with a look and marched them to the car like she was fleeing sure disaster. In her hurry, she failed to notice the four new tires on her car, and Jason watching from the front window.

Julie noticed because she saw the tires gleaming brightly in the porch light. She walked around the car and wondered if their fairy godmother had found them at last on the farm. She knew that Sarah had spent her last extra hundred on gravel for the long drive after the wash-out in May. Sarah was so frugal that she'd stopped filling the prescription for anti-anxiety medication because she said they were too expensive. Julie had waited for the breakdown that she hoped Sarah wouldn't have as she weaned herself off the pills.

Julie looked at the shiny sidewalls again and felt sick. She hoped the tires weren't the result of a dangerous blowout and a credit card splurge. Walking through the orderly, clean house, she marveled over the force of her little sister. Julie sat on the bed next to her sister and rubbed her arm to wake her, "Hey, sleepyhead. Are you holding out on me? Where'd you get the cash for the tires?"

Sarah came out of another dream of dancing with Jason Lambert. He kept trying to give her plane tickets for Boston, New York and Paris. She was considering Paris when she opened her eyes. She gave Julie a sleepy smile, "The kids were great last night, Julie. And the Lamberts brought me in to the dining room to show me off to their friends. It was nice for a change."

Julie sat patiently waiting for Sarah to process her first question, "Tires? Don't tell me I have a flat!" She shot out of bed with that thought.

At three-thirty in the morning, the Monroe sisters walked around the car, looked at each other and shook their heads. Sarah grumped, "It must have been Jason Lambert."

Julie laughed, "Jeez, Sarah. I thought you said that man didn't like you. What have you done to him?" If she could have breathed out heart-shaped bubbles she would have.

"Arch romantic! The man can't stand me. He has told me to go home to Boston so many times, I am nearly convinced to pack up and go." She touched the shiny rubber with her toe and then looked up at the starlit sky above the farm. "Now I owe him," she reverted back to wariness.

56

"Sarah, when I met him yesterday, I was in shock. First, you never told me how horribly scarred the poor man is, and second, you never insinuated that the children know him and like him. I think you have him all wrong." Julie was suspicious of Sarah's reaction to the man.

"If anyone has if wrong, it is Jason Lambert. I wonder what he was thinking." Sarah slipped back into bed and tried to fall asleep until 4:30 because Maggie had told her not to arrive until five. Maggie expected everyone to sleep in late and could start the day alone. Sarah was wide awake and worried about Jason Lambert and his urge to help her by scolding her. She pulled on her running shoes and stepped off the porch stretching. By four-thirty, she had a path of flattened grass in the back meadow. At the end of the summer, the children began to refer to that field as "Worries Track" because Sarah started running when she had problems to worry.

By six-thirty that first day of Worries Track, her skin had lost its flushed heat, but her body hummed from the exertion of running a half-marathon first thing in the morning. Jason stood behind her and figured her prizefighter bounce was due to the praise of the evening before; he liked her new confidence. "Good morning, Sarah. Did the children settle down and go right to bed?"

She nodded gravely. "They had a wonderful time." She turned around holding a bowl of blueberry juice that she'd just squeezed. She was surprised that he stood before her in his cotton pajamas and a robe. She suddenly felt a rush of attraction probably supplied by Julie's romantic hints that morning. She continued stirring in the cornstarch she'd just added to the juice to thicken it.

His eyes fell to her hands and then traveled slowly up to her lips. He sighed and took a step back.

Sarah blurted out, "Mr. Lambert, thank you for the tires. I really can't afford them." She placed the blueberry filling on the table and dropped each fresh blueberry into it one at a time. He must have stepped forward to watch her because she thought she felt his heat at her back. Everything in her wanted to back up, but she steadied her hands and placed them flat on the counter before her.

His words were quiet and nearly whispered, "Sarah. Turn around and speak to me." One of his hands rested beside hers on the counter.

Sarah sighed and breathed out an explanation, "I didn't ignore you about the tires out of stubbornness. I used all my extra money for gravel after parts of our road washed out in May. Please take the money for the tires out of my pay."

"Look at me," his voice was now harsh, so she turned slightly to find him blue-eyed and angry yet again. "Let's clear something up this morning, Miss High and Mighty Goddess of Pastry and Grand Silences." She tried to back away and bumped into the counter. It made her blink. She was conscious of Maggie reentering the kitchen. His voice was harsh, "I enjoy speaking with your children and find them much more unaffected than you. The new tires and brakes were for them, so you don't kill them the next time you decide to drive home in the rain. Jesus, Sarah! And I do not want you to go home to Boston. Home is here, got that?" His eyes fell to her mouth which was trembling, and he started forward to kiss her but stopped himself in time.

He pushed himself from the counter and stalked out of the kitchen without his coffee. Sarah tried to go back to preparing the tarts but wept until she couldn't breathe and paced in front of her station wringing her shaking hands. Maggie hushed her, patted her back and finally sent Sarah out to the garden to walk after Sarah baked an entire tray of misshapen turnovers.

A half-hour later, Isabel Lambert called down to ask Maggie to have breakfast with her. "Why is our pastry chef running laps in her bare feet outside the equestrian exercise yard?"

Maggie wryly laughed, "Sarah is training for a marathon to benefit runaway girls." Then she rolled her eyes and confessed the scene before breakfast to her oldest friend. She added that Jason was reportedly acting like a raging beast in the lab. He hadn't eaten a thing for breakfast. The two, older women grinned at each other and agreed it was going tolerably well for an odd romance.

That afternoon they received a long distance phone call from Boston for a "Miss Sarah Monroe." Her old boss was on the warpath and headed in their direction. That skunk of a chef Michel de Gault had remembered the name "Jennings" from accolades for Majorane in Boston. He phoned the restaurant that morning to tell Jennings that Sarah was passing off his recipes as her own. One of Sarah's former coworkers called to warn her that David Jennings was on his way to Lambertville. When Sarah heard this through Lou, she began to laugh out loud and completely regained her equilibrium. She cooked for the rest of the day quietly and apologized to Maggie for the upset of the morning.

Maggie had watched the ebb and flow of Sarah's moods for two months. She stopped Sarah before they left for the day. Maggie placed a hand on Sarah's arm and squeezed gently as they stood in the employee parking lot at the back of the research building. Maggie eyed the new tires and tried to placate Sarah but give some sense to Jason's overwrought concern, "He was always a gentle, quiet person as a child. His brother Stephen drew him out." She looked out to the clouds hanging over the mountain. "He likes you, Sarah. He is just terrible at expressing it." Maggie bit her lip and asked quietly, "Did anyone ever tell you about the accident?"

Sarah blushed as all the hints hit her, "Bad tires on a slick road? Oh my!" Her heart hurt for him.

Maggie nodded, "She was just a normal woman with her child in a little, raggedy car on a slick road. She skidded right into the passenger side of Jason's car and killed his wife on impact. Both cars spun out of control and his tumbled. There was a fire, and he was burned getting Chloe out."

"No wonder he is so angry. I am too eager to haul them all over the county like he says." Sarah raised her eyes to the building thinking about his words more objectively. "I'm used to fitting so much in a day from living in the city. If I keep them busy, they don't find trouble. I am trying to adjust."

Maggie squeezed her hand and told her the accident oc-curred nearly three years ago and then added, "You are a very young woman to manage those little souls so well. You should see yourself light up when you talk about the children or about the farm. Sarah, I hope you realize that you do belong here, no matter what anyone says." Maggie's gray eyes misted just a bit thinking of the harsh words uttered by Jason.

"Thank you, Miss Maggie. I am fortunate to be here," Sarah nodded, slipped behind the wheel and escaped the Lamberts for the evening. Jason watched from his office as her little car turned left at the main road and imagined her taking the turn on two wheels. His heart lurched at his clumsiness with her, so he began to plot out his next entreaty for her affection.

CHAPTER 6

Visitor

Chef David Jennings was a dapper giant of a man with a daring shock of white-blond hair gelled into daring spikes. He stood with hands on hips in a light blue suit, black shirt and silver bolero tie when the staff looked up at his shout of a laugh from the screened back door.

Sarah giggled when she spotted him surveying the kitchen from the doorway like the god he thought he was to cooking. Her voice was coy, and Maggie's head snapped up to hear Sarah use such a tone, "Chef Jennings, you look like a movie matinee cowboy. This is West Virginia not Texas!" She slipped her dish into the oven and launched herself into his arms. He was wide-eyed but genuinely amused. Sarah kissed him on the cheek as Jason appeared in the doorway. Isabel called from the front room worried that security had noticed an intruder. Sarah cast introductions among them with a blush spreading from her cheeks to throat.

Maggie wagged a finger at David and Sarah, "No defections to the north, Sarah. Straighten this great big, handsome man out and send him home."

Sarah faced David with an evil glint in her eye. Jason was intrigued by his quiet Sarah looking animated and daring. "There was no need for you to come all this way," she said, but the pleasure was all too apparent in her voice.

David Jennings laughed and wagged his finger back at Maggie, "So you are the fire-breathing dragon, Chef Margaret Turner. My compliments for dispensing with that idiot de Gault!" He extended a hand to Maggie, "I am David Jennings, former warden of this scrumptious thing." He tossed his head toward Sarah who rolled her eyes. His eyes glittered over the hostile glare from Jason who stood blocking in the doorway, "I just had to see how my best intern in ten years escaped me and was reborn a renowned scandal." He also explained that he was traveling south to meet with his partner in Charleston. He raised a brow at Sarah, "And Georgiana sent me with a few boxes from your apartment."

David took a step forward to shake hands with Jason Lambert and examine the man thoroughly. David glanced back to Maggie and Sarah with a grin, "Michel de Gault's phone message was hysterical! We played it for the whole staff. You used a variation on your Italian dishes, didn't you?" He squeezed Sarah and kissed her temple after she nodded. "My darling dilettante of the kitchen, you have true talent that you waste. Sarah, tell these very trusting people where you learned those recipes. Let's see, I'll bet you wowed them with pasta primavera, rusticana fagiolo and semolina Bolognese." He winked at Jason and Maggie and then added, "She did the same thing to me and then rubbed my nose in their humble beginnings."

Sarah tilted up her chin, "Truly, Chef Jennings, what I made for the service was dictated by the ingredients de Gault left after his meltdown. I wanted them to compliment the better dishes prepared by the rest of the staff." She sighed and gave in to his cocked eyebrow, "I supported myself during graduate school by cooking at the college cafeteria. I made a version of those dishes once a week for two years straight. It was the only thing I could think of doing with the mess Michel left us. Please don't be angry." Her eyes glittered over to Jason's confused look.

Jason wasn't confused by the food or the tripe about the dishes being knock-offs of cafeteria food. He was examining the interplay between Jennings and Sarah. At first he thought they were lovers; she was so warm and tender with this man. As they spoke about his restaurant and Maggie's kitchen, he realized they were colleagues who respected each other.

David shifted on his feet, looked around at the large kitchen and leered at Jason and Maggie, "Well, now I understand why you're here, Sarah darling. I was appalled at the size of the farm. You said it was small and dilapidated, but how will you keep up with the grass alone? I enjoyed the tour of the vegetable garden given by Leanne—it's showing well for your efforts. The children are adorable—if you like children," he wrinkled his nose, "and your very pretty sister is a flirt, but this is just sweet." He nodded at Maggie, "May I take her out for a walk? I noticed a lovely garden with a fountain. I won't steal her away." David made it obvious that he was more of a mentor or older brother.

Maggie shook her head, "No—no more interruptions today. Cook with us today, Chef Jennings. I would like to learn something from a famous maestro." She put on her stern kitchen face. "Jason, do you need something?"

David looked from Jason to Maggie and back. He whistled a low note. Shucking his jacket, he accepted the apron that Sarah produced with docile efficiency, "I believe Mr. Lambert and I will have some time to speak this evening. Yes, Jason?"

Jason smiled at Sarah's odd look between them and nodded at Jennings who was a surprise in person. Jason had worried that he might have to drug Sarah to keep her from going back to Boston with the suave voice on the phone. David shocked them all by saying, "If this little girl passes her CPA exam and leaves the kitchen, I am coming back down here to kidnap her. I'm serious, Sarah. You may dabble with accounting, but your heart is in the kitchen. You are just beginning to show your talent."

Sarah smiled at all of them and muttered, "Promises, promises. Let's get the lunch service together. Miss Maggie? Assignments?"

Maggie grinned, "Rescue whatever you threw in the oven. David, show me what you would do with this miserable pork loin." She stood poised to season the thing into submission. David grinned at the challenge as he tied his apron and prepared to spar with the old woman.

When Lou and Billy came in that afternoon, Billy took one look at David and drawled under his breath, "Who's the big gay guy in the kitchen? Get that flamer away from my station!" Sarah could not keep a straight face as David flirted furiously with the old man.

Lou shook his head and raised a brow at Sarah. During

her one o'clock break, she took David Jennings for a turn in the garden. Lou could not stop grinning with relief that Sarah was really not about to leave them for her former position at the prestigious restaurant. He hoped that her sister and Jason finally understood what she gave up when she left Boston in May.

David and Sarah walked the garden during her short break. "Has your sister heard anything from her husband? We could hire a detective." David Jennings looked around the old gardens with wide-spreading fruit trees at the outer edge, a winding section of roses and a pond with a fountain in the center.

"There's no word and no extra funds for an investigator." Sarah lowered her voice a bit, "Julie owes more than I do from the institute." She blushed and looked away because she'd just reviewed all of the family mail that had barely been opened for months. "It's enough to keep the children happy right now."

The big man lost his blousy persona and became serious, "I understand staying for the children. I hadn't realized how young they were when we talked before you left. But Sarah, you cannot give up everything for your sister and her mistakes." He frowned, "She says you are planning to open a tax business in town?"

Sarah shook her head, "It's one of Julie's pipedreams. She's pushing the CPA exam which I agree I should take now while I'm ready to prepare for it. I don't know that I want to be an accountant."

He shook his head, "You love to cook. Why is it obvious to everyone but your sister that you need the regiment of the kitchen? Sweetheart, I hope you are taking care of yourself. How are your nerves?"

The reference to her bouts of anxiousness made Sarah pale, "I'm creating my own routines here." She looked up into his face and saw genuine concern, "I weaned myself off of the pills. They made me too . . . ." She searched for the right word.

"Dull? Sometimes you worked an entire shift like a zombie." He winced when her face hardened into a glare. He shook his head. "I am not your boss anymore, Sarah. I am concerned.

I want you back in Boston but not teetering on the edge of burn-out like you were."

"I managed this 'anxiety disorder' that they love to label and treat with anti-depressants for a long time before Georgiana took me to that clinic. Those pills calmed me down, but they also stole any real feelings. Real life hurts, David Jennings." She was surprised at the grin on his face as her irritation flared.

"And real life is full of joy—the taste and the smell of which you understand. Be angry with me, but every good sense is telling me to lure you off your beloved mountain and take you home to Boston. Use your gifts, Sarah."

Sarah grimaced, "You sound just like my father. He was always telling me to find my own way, but I didn't understand. I remember wanting to be like my sister. Julie was so beautiful and easy with everyone."

"A paltry talent next to yours. Don't give up the kitchen in your new life, Sarah." He made a little straightening gesture that signaled the end of this interview, "I could recommend a few restaurants in Wheeling or further south if you leave this position." He looked up to the façade of the older portion of the mansion where a man stood watching them walk. The man's silvery hair gleamed in the afternoon sun because his head was bowed to watch them.

Sarah tilted her head at David Jennings. She didn't know what to make of his visit or his advice. Georgiana Ensky, her friend and the restaurant's hostess, had often teased her about Chef Jennings' favoritism with her. While he scolded Sarah about her part-time status at the culinary school, he took the time to teach her techniques that he had honed over twenty years of cooking and managing kitchens. He had discouraged any talk of an accounting position, yet he had come to her with a knotty problem last year when he found his bookkeeper's records a torturous mess.

In notes since she left Boston for Lilac Hill, Chef Jennings had insisted that she was welcome to return to Boston. During their walk, he offered her references that might open doors in

Wheeling or further south to Charleston where his partner's business was located. He offered to help her finance a restaurant of her own when she was ready. Standing in the Lambert's garden, Sarah impulsively hugged him, "I'm not ready yet. You have to trust that I know my limits."

David Jennings wagged a finger at Sarah, "You're gaining confidence. I can see that. We'll let your future rest for the moment."

He cocked a brow and glanced at his watch, "They're having a quality control issue in Charleston. I want to arrive at the restaurant during dinner service. I also promised to speak to Jason Lambert before I left. Interesting man!"

When they returned to the house, they found the kitchen deserted, and everyone milling in the hall leading to the large siting room in the residence portion of the house. Lou whispered, "Miss Isabel might be having a heart attack." Most of the staff was dithering around preparing for her to be rushed to the hospital. Glimpsing into the room, Sarah saw Maggie Turner tending to Isabel while Joseph Lambert spoke on phone. Between instructions to Maggie, Joseph was muttering, "I'm so sorry."

Jason rushed into the room. He knelt beside her partially prone body and picked up his mother's hand. He frowned down into her tear-streaked face and asked gently, "Mother, what's wrong? How can I help?" Isabel clutched at her chest and abdomen but shook her head as tears fell.

At a look from Jason, the staff backed up from the doorway and reassembled itself out of habit. The house staff could wait for the paramedics, so the kitchen staff returned to complete the dinner service whether it was eaten or not. Sarah walked David Jennings to the back door and let him go. "I'll call you if I change my mind. Thank you." Sarah returned to the kitchen, but Lou pointed at Maggie's vacated station. Sarah nodded and took over the head chef's dishes.

By the next morning, Joseph Lambert assembled the staff and announced, "Miss Isabel is being treated for heart palpitations and stress. She will return from the hospital today." Back in the privacy of the kitchen, Maggie grumbled over Joseph's penchant for drama and overdone announcements. Sarah wondered what could have panicked Isabel who exuded an air of serenity and gentle humor.

After David Jennings' advice, Sarah worried about choices his visit had kindled. She was unsettled about leaving the children and her sister alone at the farmhouse on Lilac Hill. She wanted to teach the children to survive better than her sister had during their first years without support of their parents. Sarah did not want them spoiled and insulated from real life, but they were too young for full awareness of the poverty that seemed to hang like a threat at the end of every month.

She revisited memories of her blond-haired, handsome father giving her pep talks before tests and other challenges. Her heart warmed and ached when she realized that she could remember the content, but his voice was now indistinct and melded with David Jennings and Jason Lambert's deep tones.

CHAPTER 7

Jason's Mistake

Jason Lambert was bluntly honest with his mother and usually failed to understand that three-year-old Chloe listened and understood most of their conversations. The little girl might seem to be playing with dolls or coloring, but she had become an expert on the relationship between her father and the rest of the world. Chloe understood that he did not look like her even-featured grandfather or Uncle Stephen. He did not look like broad, handsome Lou who had two, loud boys older than her in elementary school. Her father did not have features even like the old man who gardened with Joe whom she loved with the infatuation of all young females for tanned, olive-skinned gods like the young Mexican man might be. But her father was the most attractive man on the planet to Chloe because he loved her so deeply it hurt.

He let her touch the furrows of the leftover skin on his face from pulling it together imperfectly after the metal had sliced him to the bone. The furrows ran from his hairline, across his left temple and crossed over his cheek and down to his chin. Chloe told him it was his river of life and made up stories like a palm reader; sometimes her words made his eyes water. She ran her fingers down his neck where the glass nearly sliced the artery that she told him was the jugular, but he rarely let her touch the burns on his chest from diving back into the wreck to pull her infant seat from the car.

Her mother had died instantly, he told her. He let her see pictures of a beautiful blonde on the arm of a man with plain, regular features. She knew he kept her mother's favorite dresses and her jewelry, so Chloe might enjoy knowing that part of her mother one day. He didn't know she hung on his every word. She digested his worries and opinions until they boiled and erupted at the oddest moments.

Sarah was feeling comfortable as they made sugar cookies for a little party Chloe wanted to organize for her father. He had been working on a difficult contract and was finally finished. The dinner party the night before had been an extravagant affair with customers who came to accept the finished product. Sarah had allowed Julie's three children to stay in the playroom with other employees' children who hadn't arranged babysitting for the extra hours. She thought about getting a dog or a cat with the extra bonus from the overtime and loosened up into an adventure story about her old dog. Trenton was still a happy place in her memory when their large shepherd had been alive.

Out of sight in the hallway, Jason listened to Sarah's little story of hooking a sled to the great beast one winter. Chloe asked questions and decorated the cookies they'd cut out with colored sugar. As they finished, he hesitated just a moment too long. Chloe's question quieted the other conversations in the kitchen, as she sliced to the core with her high, innocent voice, "Miss Sarah, do all of the Monroe children have different fathers like your three? You and your sister look nothing alike." Chloe blinked at Sarah's open mouth because in nearly four-year-old abstraction, she had meditated on how similar Robby, Leanne and Annabelle seemed despite their diverse parentage. Their names and appearances had been a topic of conversation between Isabel and Jason and then a lively speculation among adults in the playroom last night as Chloe played with the Monroe children.

Sarah's voice was a shocked whisper, "My three?" Her brain ceased functioning. Her first impulse was to throw all the cookies onto the floor. The pan wobbled in her hand. She gulped down a breath, lifted the tray higher and deposited it in the oven. Maggie and Lou stood with gaping mouths at the entrée station poised over steak for that evening. Billy groaned a little curse and continued cutting vegetables.

Chloe commented when her question went unanswered, unabashed at the gaff, "Daddy says It's a shame you haven't a man at the farm, and that you must be doing the best you can. Are you?" She blinked up to Sarah in innocence.

Sarah shook out a breath that wanted to level some sarcasm onto the little girl. Chloe was just repeating like a little parrot. Pity filled Sarah for all of them in this tableau, "Chloe, each of those children had a father who loved their mother; fathers who loved their babies when they were born. People die too soon; sometimes marriages don't work, but the children should not suffer for it." Even Sarah was surprised at how calm and patient her voice sounded in the silent kitchen. Chloe's eyes widened with understanding, and Sarah regretted her last thought.

Jason came from behind Chloe and stood in the doorway; he began to apologize, but Sarah held up a hand to stop him. "Your Daddy is here for a walk. Aren't you, Mr. Lambert? I'll have the cookies delivered when they finish cooling." Sarah turned her back and began cleaning up her station. She didn't care about any of the town's opinions of Julie, but she had never considered the prejudice from implied illegitimacy. She hadn't even considered any cruelty like that might plague the children. She felt color rise into her cheeks and burn there. Her blood thrummed through her veins and blocked any sound for a few minutes. Someone was talking, and she whirled around to find out who could be speaking with tears blinding her. She dashed the moisture away with her apron.

Jason Lambert stood there talking in an empty kitchen. He must have ordered the staff away with one look. Maggie had picked up Chloe and stood on the patio beyond the screen door waiting for the explosion to occur. Sarah shook her head and shouted at the pleading man, "Stop talking. I can't hear you. I'm so upset. I can't hear anything." Each word was pronounced in careful, even syllables that might cost her all control to utter. Jason sucked in an anxious breath. Sarah's complete undoing was right there in the afternoon kitchen in the middle of preparation for dinner service.

Her fingers twitched over violence. Steam rising from a boiling pot on one of the burners caught her eye. Billy's discarded knife gleamed on the cutting board. A full roll of panic threatened to shatter all her firm edges and spring apart her tight control. She sipped in one breath of the moist heat of the afternoon kitchen and made herself exhale.

Sarah stepped away from Jason and opened the oven to check on the pan of cats and dogs. She regretted the story about Captain, her long-dead German shepherd. The gentle good feeling that came with telling the tale had made her soft and vulnerable. She regretted agreeing to teach Chloe how to bake. How could she let herself enjoy another little child, his child, and expect to remain intact? She felt branded by all of Julie's impetuous mistakes.

Sarah moved in the automatic impulse of the kitchen as she checked the boiling pot—the potatoes were nearly ready. Words left her in a mutter, "It's a wonder they have any friends from the town. I can't believe they even let us attend Sunday services! I had no idea!" A sob of building panic bubbled in her chest.

Jason Lambert watched Sarah pace before her station, check Maggie's day list on the board and wring her hands in her apron. A glance at the clock and one larger gulp of oxygen quickly expelled, she peeked at the cookies again and removed them. Shoulders pinned back, she stepped toward the kitchen door, "Chloe, come on in here, honey." Her lifted voice was rusty from swallowing hurt. She left the doorway when Maggie brought the child back into the room with a worried look at Sarah.

Sarah glanced up to a devastated Jason Lambert, "Chloe needs to learn how to remove them from the pan, sir. Warm sugar cookies are about as fragile as the human heart."

Sarah decided to find Michael Elliott after the panic attack over the town's opinion of Julie's motley crew of children. She could tell herself to toughen up during the day, but her worries woke her in the middle of the night and throttled her. In those few minutes in the Lambert kitchen, she had discovered that a mother's love was made, not born. She was drowning in love for Robby, Leanne, Annabelle and now little Chloe. Nothing should invite hurt on any of those children. In renewed silence, she reasoned it all out as she reviewed all of the paperwork from Julie's chaotic life.

Michael had filed to legally adopt Julie's elder two children before he left. Thompson, Leanne's deadbeat daddy, had actually been cordial when Sarah visited with the paperwork on a trip through town to see old friends a year ago. He had apologized to Sarah for being such a drunken wreck that it had cost her a semester at school. She remembered keeping her tense countenance in place during that meeting, but she realized that he had been expecting something different. He was probably relieved that Julie had never sued for the court-ordered child support or alimony. Sarah doubted that he even cared that his child and ex-wife were living in West Virginia.

Sarah wondered if the town considered the children well-mannered angels or an unruly blight. She worried about the town's opinion of the Monroe sisters of Lilac Hill. Julie was sweet and unaffected if slightly unknown except at the grocery. Sarah had exposed the children to public scrutiny by taking them to church, visiting the park and frequenting the library. Robby had made friends during his first few months at the town elementary school, and Leanne would start kindergarten in a few weeks. When Sarah took them into town for shopping or church, she cautiously observed other people's reactions. A deep reserve sheltered her and made her introspective.

A week after the disastrous question over sugar cookies, Sarah concluded that it was only Jason Lambert who held such an opinion of the Monroe sisters. She was shocked that he let Julie's children talk to his Chloe at all and settled into a dispirited silence in the kitchen that no amount of good-natured nudging would unbend. Billy told all of them to leave her alone; Sarah Monroe was obviously working on a problem only she could solve.

Sarah took a part-time job making desserts for a little restaurant in Wheeling to pay for a new private investigator to look into Michael Elliott's disappearance. The job let her drive away from Lambertville for the whole weekend if she stayed with her elderly cousins. She felt hollow and rusty for most of August, as the weather turned dry and hot. Sometimes when she ran that month, she thought she heard the earth drumming hollow under her pounding feet. Everyone prayed for rain, but Sarah prayed for some information or word about Michael. His signature could give the children one name as a shield against public humiliation.

Bending to Julie's urging, Sarah also registered to take the CPA exam in October. Starting a business was a far reach for a cook with a flair for pastry, but Julie kept talking about how much the mine would pay a new CPA if they could lure one who might last. Sarah found the job at the Lambert's mansion excruciating now that she knew Jason's true opinion of the Monroe sisters. Whenever he came to the kitchen and stood at the counter with Maggie talking about trivialities, Sarah avoided his eyes and kept working. Chloe came and went on a regular basis asking safe questions. The little girl made miniature meals for her doll friends on a tiny silver platter like her grandmother enjoyed. Sarah sometimes wanted to comfort the little girl like she did Annabelle, but she kept herself steady and removed.

CHAPTER 8

The Fire Break

Julie cautioned Sarah against paying the investigator any more money by the third week in August. There had been a lead in Utah, but it had died out when the man found there denied ever even driving through West Virginia. The letter from the investigator was still fluttering under a vase of wildflowers on the dining room table with the mail a week after it arrived.

Sarah had quit the job in Wheeling because it was so expensive to drive her little car all the way there and back, and she'd realized repairs would be too expensive if it broke down. So she played with the children all weekend, visited the library in town and attended a few of the town's concerts which were often sponsored by the Lamberts. It was interesting to see them all dressed up without preparing food for the party. Everybody danced or sang along with the songs they knew, ate ice cream or snow cones and sat in loose family groups.

Sarah watched the Lamberts out of the corner of her eye but stuck to the friends she had made the first two weeks in May through Robby's school group. If Chloe and Leanne talked, she might be on the periphery, but she really did not want to infringe on the gentry's time. That's what the bitterness of Jason Lambert's opinion had created in her mind; she was deemed a servant with shabby morals and unkempt children while the Lamberts acted like royalty. She knew it was unfair and that the Lamberts had proven over and again how generous and kind they were, but Sarah draped on bitterness like a gauzy scarf.

The night of the ice cream social in August, Julie had taken the weekend to stay with their cousins, so Sarah took the children out just for the diversion. The long days of August reminded her of the new school year, but this time, she would not return to the cold north. She missed her second floor apartment, her friends and the old college buildings.

While the children ate their ice cream, Walt Stone asked Sarah to dance. He was one of Julie's only remaining friends from her marriage to Michael Elliott. Sarah had worn a long, layered skirt and a sheer, flirty top on a whim. With her hair piled up in the heat, she felt like another person dancing with a handsome man who reminded her again of a cowboy with his western shirt, long sideburns and arched, dark brows. While they danced, Sarah waved to her collection of children.

Walt pulled her a little closer and asked, "Do you ever go out?"

Sarah smiled because he was so awkward and said, "I might if the right guy asked."

Then he blundered like so many of the men Sarah had known and asked her if she "liked to party." Something in Sarah froze as she continued to look up to Walt's inviting leer down her blouse.

She shook her head and told him, "You are barking up the wrong tree. I am not a 'party' type of girl." She tried to smile at him, but her mouth trembled.

He looked down at her, grew serious and remained quiet for the rest of the dance. He walked away disgusted after the dance ended. He told his friends that he had "really blown it" with Sarah Monroe after waiting the whole summer to talk to her alone. Despite her Jersey girl curves and flirty walk, she was a lady all the way through, and he had insulted her with his clumsiness.

Jason, his brother Stephen and the second shift cook Lou listened to this report and shrugged at Walt and his friends. The younger men concluded it was obvious that Sarah Monroe did not view anyone in the Lambertville vicinity worth a second look. Lou grumbled something about "stupid young men" and crossed the floor to ask her out for a serious romp as his wife clapped and hollered.

The children joined in and with changing partners, Sarah found herself dancing with Jason Lambert after a few months of not seeing him at all. She was surprised at how well they moved together though he didn't try to speak to her like Walt did. She winked at Leanne who was looking dreamily at the two of them. He smiled and the little girl hid her face as Chloe laughed.

Jason started calmly, "Walt Stone didn't mean any harm, Sarah. He was just making conversation, and you probably stonewalled him into saying something stupid." He was not holding her as closely as Walt, but Sarah was more aware of his hands and the heat meeting between them.

She knew she should act haughty, but it fell away in curiosity, "Stonewalled him?" she glanced nervously over to where Walt and his friends watched the dancing. She sneered slightly. They might be tossing the beers back and acting confident, but Sarah could see the false bravado from across the room. She wondered how men could get to their ages and not feel more comfortable in their own skins. She knew she was accustomed to hers and slid bolder eyes back to look directly at Jason Lambert in his scolding mode.

Jason nodded, "Yeah, that silent thing you do, so a person doesn't know where he stands." His hand found the small of her back, and he realized he had tensed his hand into a fist. He relaxed it and pressed her just a touch closer.

She was still looking up at him mesmerized, "Silent thing? I told that man I wasn't a party girl. I may not know much about West Virginia or Lambertville, sir, but 'partying' in my neck of the woods includes drinking, drugs and promiscuity. I think he was pretty clear." She smiled up at him as his eyes widened perceptively.

"I'm just saying that Walt Stone is not a bad guy, Sarah. I hear he was a good friend to Michael Elliott." Jason considered her upturned face and struggled not to forget his scars. He could forget that she worked in his kitchen, but he couldn't deny that she was married and devoted to her little children. Jason stopped talking and lured her back to the dance. They finished the song and changed partners a number of times. When he walked her to her car later, a bit of a thaw had begun.

The alarm that sounded after the one o'clock break was

not like any other Sarah had heard previously. Her hands were full of bread dough for dinner service, and some pastry dough waited for apple dumplings Joseph Lambert wanted with dinner. Her mind was chocked full of numbers and formulas for the CPA exam. She'd taken a few financial advising appointments through Julie's connections and worried because her business license had not arrived. She had broached changing all the children's names to "Monroe" last night and had shared angry words with Julie. Julie didn't care about public opinion or Jason Lambert's prejudice.

Billy set aside his prep work, covered everything with wrap and tossed the bowls into the fridge. "Cover that, Sarah. That was the fire alarm. I thought I saw smoke on the ridge earlier, so I called the rangers to investigate." He ran a hand over his face and took off his apron. Maggie and Lou returned from a meeting with the housekeeping staff a moment later. As a team, they joined the gardeners and then the yardmen.

Sarah was surprised as Jason's secretary and all of his technicians joined them on the lawn. They hurried to the barn a half mile away as Sarah saw the billows of smoke rise from the thickly wooded crest of Lilac Hill. Her heart pounded as Maggie hesitated to allow the children to go out to the firebreak when shovels and rakes were distributed.

The elder Lamberts were in Raleigh on business, and the daycare workers were young and needed to man the breaks. Billy said something about sending Sarah back to the house with the children. Jason snapped. He was angry at the suggestion. "She needs to know what it is to live out here just like the children do. If it's dangerous, we'll send the children back to the house first." He included Sarah in the same category as the children.

In teams, they spread out along the firebreak that Billy said had been dug out a year ago and cleared it of any debris that might catch fire. They worked for about two hours until the little children started to complain. When another alarm sounded, and they started digging the trench wider, Jason gave the order for the women and children to return to the house.

Sarah asked Maggie to call her sister at the farm and ask her if there was any sign of fire there. Sarah donned the wet kerchief that Billy offered her as her eyes watered when the smoke blew down the hill.

By four o'clock, the firebreak had been widened twice its original width, but Sarah was sobered by the loud explosions at the top of the mountain. Lou explained that the pine trees heated from the bottom layer of dried needles and exploded once the sap boiled. The light breeze that delivered the layer of thin smoke down the hillside would also fan the fire according to one of the gardeners. When Jason walked to their part of the line, he roughly pulled the shovel out of Sarah's hand and pointed toward the house. She took the shovel back and nodded. She heard a loud discussion among her team featuring her name and then Lou laughing as she started to jog halfway through the walk back to the main house.

When she burst through the kitchen door, she found that Maggie had finished the dinner with Jason's secretary and Maura, Stephen's eldest daughter. Even the apple dumplings were baking. Sarah intended to wash, change clothes and finish her shift, but Maggie started talking about the state road and possible closures.

Maggie was worried over the road because the elder Lambert's were due home, and she hoped they weren't delayed. She called the sheriff's office and found out that the county road was still open, but crews had been dispatched to check the entire area. Maggie said that her sister Julie was calling to ask the Stones in Lambertville to keep the children while she worked the evening shift. Maggie rolled her eyes and said, "If it was my farm, I'd be out there protecting it."

Moments later as Sarah's little car flew up the drive and out to the main road, Maggie groaned at her thoughtless words. When Jason and the rest of the staff filed in heated and dirty an hour later, it took Maggie a full half-hour to build the nerve to tell him that Sarah had left for home. He cursed and called the farm, cursed again because a fifteen minute drive had taken her more than an hour. Still on the phone as his parents arrived, he cursed Sarah thoroughly, "You are so impetuous and selfish."

Sarah replied, "I have more than your good opinion to worry over because the fire is on the way down the mountain, and I can't see the back cottage for the smoke. The road crew that had promised to follow me home when they could, haven't arrived yet." Jason gathered a team of men who weren't entirely spent, kissed Chloe good night and climbed into the Lou's SUV to drive around to the other side of smoldering Lilac Hill.

The team of men were worried over their little pastry chef and her collection of children but ran into the same problems she had. They were pressed into working with the sheriff's crew at the crossroads first. That group slapped the Lambert men on their backs about worrying over the dark-haired spitfire who could shovel like a man and insisted in driving her little car over the trenches to get home. They had been the ones to call the mine for help at Julie and Sarah Monroe's farm. The sheriff told them to turn around because the mine had trucked up a backhoe and a stout team of men, but Lou patted Jason on the back and said, "I think the boss would like to see this for himself."

When they climbed out of the valley, the sun was hanging low on the horizon, and the fire above the rim of the forest could be seen for miles. It glowed more ferociously than it had in bright daylight. Lou mumbled something about the fire of 1974 when two farms and thousands of acres burned. Billy grouched that it didn't look as bad as all that. He reminded the two men that they'd been no more than boys at the time like Stephen's Maura who was now eleven.

Jason nearly turned Lou around when he saw the crew working the back field of Monroe Farm. Sarah and Julie were out in the field closest to the woods overseeing the fire line, but men larger than them had taken their shovels and forced them to stand out of the way. Julie had been crying for some time over her helplessness with the raging fire that was smoldering in the woods way up the mountain.

When Jason saw Sarah, really saw Sarah with her hands on

her hips and Annabelle wrapped around one leg, he thought he might collapse in utter humility. She wasn't distressed or upset by the fire. The young woman was energized by the challenge of the live thing on the mountain. She ran to Lou and gave him a hug after scooping up little Annabelle, "I bet none of you ate dinner. Julie and I just fed the crew the last of our leftovers, but we can make omelets. Come inside the house before it's a cinder." She was fresh from a shower in clean jeans and a tee-shirt. She looked ready to run a mile. Billy was the only one with any sense, "Sure Sarah. I've always been curious about your farmhouse on Lilac Hill. I'll give you a hand."

Jason waited to speak to her until they had all washed, eaten quickly and returned to the porch to check the progress of the fire. Julie walked Lou and Billy back out to the SUV, and the children were sent up to prepare for bed. Jason dared to stand next to Sarah, as she concentrated on the crews finishing and mobilizing for the trip back to the mine with the small bulldozer on a low trailer. His voice was ragged, "Sarah, I apologize."

She looked up to him in the half-dark and shook her head, "You just call them like you see them, Mr. Lambert. Julie and I had no idea what we were doing when we signed the deed for this place. We had just buried my father, and the paperwork came in the mail. It was familiar from a few vacations when we were kids, and the area seemed safer than Trenton. You just can't run from reality, can you?" She was thinking that the fire was like the sweeping sorrow that kept plaguing her.

Jason agreed though he had wanted to propel his apology forward with all the sincerity he could muster and end their constant feud. "When I agreed to sell this place, I thought Elizabeth Monroe was buying it. I remembered her visiting with my father when she came to stay here."

Sarah nodded, "We had to sell the house in Trenton to pay all the bills after my father died so soon after Mom. Then there was the divorce, and Leanne's father threatening all of us. It seemed like a godsend when the sale of the Trenton house offset most of the mortgage on Lilac Hill. We didn't even think; just made an appointment with the estate lawyer, signed the papers to transfer ownership and sent the check. Pretty stupid, just like you keep reminding me. We were thinking about vacations here, not real life."

Jason was quiet for a moment at the ill fit of the entire story. Why would Sarah leave the children with Julie even for a short while and go back to Boston for college? It didn't fit the character of the woman who carted her babies everywhere and risked her life getting back to them tonight. "Sarah, I saw the detective's report on the sideboard when we set up for dinner. Are you still hoping Michael Elliott will come home?" He wanted to hug her to his chest and tell her to forget the man he knew only from a poor copy of his driver's license.

Sarah sighed, "Only if he wants to return. Julie thinks the children overwhelmed him, and he chose to stay away. I worry he's hurt somewhere. It's heartbreaking that he could abandon his own child, yet other men have done that," her voice fell off a little. Jason used the moment to place an arm about her shoulders. When she turned into his chest and hugged him back, Jason pulled her closer.

That night he closed his eyes and tried to forget how natural it felt to hold Sarah. Lou and Billy called their goodbyes, and Sarah stepped away and wiped her eyes. Billy took the keys to the SUV and drove them back to the Lambert mansion in silence. Jason was completely drained and heartsick over the question of Sarah Monroe.

CHAPTER 9

Healing Season

Sweet peas off the path alerted Sarah to the very end of summer just like the honeysuckle had made early summer fragrant. She gathered bouquets of them as she wandered the edges of the wood untouched by the fire. It had not crept as close to the house as Julie feared it might. She narrowed her eyes and saw the slight edges of wilting in some of the leaves: whether it heralded the end of summer or the heat of the fire was only a guess. Sarah walked the perimeter of the farm, dreamed about larger fields of crop next year and watched for signs of wildlife. Deer had invaded the corn last week, a snake had been seen investigating the barn, and there was evidence of bears digging through the compost. She snapped off a bouquet frothy white Queen Anne's lace and deposited it on the kitchen table in a mayonnaise jar to delight Julie when she finally rose.

Julie was getting better. Sarah noticed that the kitchen floor seemed cleaner first. Then the piles of sacred newspapers Julie horded were depleted in a sudden urge to have a bonfire on the gravel drive in front of the old barn. When Sarah returned home in the middle of the week after the fire, there were a few pairs of jeans, sweaters and skirts on her narrow bed, folded neatly with a note that offered them. Julie was shucking off the first layer of the heavy depression that had descended last winter and held her until July.

Sarah pulled weeds between the rows of late cabbage, beans, potatoes and turnips one morning noting the neatened condition of the other fields of flowers, herbs, peppers and cherry tomatoes. Julie had stopped dabbling at the garden and was working it in earnest.

The experimental canning of the beans, tomatoes and pepper relish on the next weekend was a comedy with Walt Stone's mother visiting to offer advice and stories. Walt and his father took Robby and Leanne to a farm fair while Annabelle worked as first assistant in the kitchen.

When the men returned with pizza, laughter bubbled through the farmhouse for the first time Sarah could remember since her father died. She watched the Stones kid with each other. Sarah listened to stories of the valley from Nancy Ann Stone and noticed that a slow joy warmed her. Julie gleamed like the golden girl she used to be at the head of the table. She caught Walt weighing the differences between the two sisters a number of times. Sarah hugged her sister as the guests pulled down the drive after dinner. Sarah whispered, "Are you happy, my dear sister?"

Julie turned to Sarah and cupped her face gently, "I knew you would make it all better, Sarah. The children are happy, the garden is joyous, and you've brought friends into the house. It's become a home, our home on Lilac Hill." Julie looked at her little sister and saw the seriousness that had fallen over Sarah who'd taken on so much responsibility. "I want you to find some joy also, Sarah. Go out with Walt. It doesn't have to be the romance of the century. He is a kind soul like you are. You have much more in common than you know."

Sarah nodded and nudged her sister playfully, "Sure. I think after this little celebration of putting up vegetables, Walt understands that I am not the 'party girl' he thought I might be." She smiled and considered his genuinely kind manner with the children and his moody silence with her. Sarah decided to make an effort to be more likeable than her normal, prickly self when she saw him next.

The first thing Jason noticed about Sarah Monroe was that her walk had changed. He'd seen her walk before in the gardens, through the kitchen and hallways at the back of the house, or her hurried gait before running past the gardens away from anger. He'd admired the easy gait she used when wandering the town gatherings with her passel of children. He had never noticed a swing in her walk before, so he narrowed his eyes and watched her skirt swing with it. He noticed she was wearing a bit of a heel, stockings and a wide skirt that brushed her legs as she paused at a window in conversation with Robby. She'd given Chloe a little wave when they passed the barbershop a moment ago because his little girl tapped on the window for her attention. He closed his eyes when Sarah disappeared into the library, and the barber moved around him, blocking the view of the window. He listened to the snip of the scissors and tried to dampen his curiosity about Sarah. Chloe was talking to her grandfather and doing a little jig to entertain him that she'd learned last week.

A man's deep voice broke through Jason's meditation on Sarah's attractive, new confidence that morning, "That Monroe girl is something else. Looking at her this morning, you'd never know she could pitch right in like a man. When she got out of her car during the fire last week and pulled on gloves, I nearly choked." Jason glanced around to see that it was the road crew foreman who had followed her back to the farm on the night of the raging wildfire on Lilac Hill.

Jason's father grunted approval, "In fact, our gardener said she worked for about four hours before that in a crew clearing the breaks on the ridge behind our place. She's quite a powerhouse." Joseph's voice held a brag that Jason usually heard when his father spoke of grandchildren and dogs. Jason smiled and winked at the barber.

Walter Stone sighed from his chair nearest the door, "She's a tough one. I was ready to put her over my knee when I found out she spread a whole load of gravel down that decrepit farm road at her place. Thick-headed woman won't ask for help and did it behind Julie's back. Julie would have had every guy at the mine up there helping. I think Sarah's bull-headed."

The barber who was cutting Jason's hair laughed, "You're just mad that she hasn't fallen all over your clumsy attempts to ask her out, Stone. With a woman like that, you need to be direct."

Jason raised an eyebrow at all of them, "Walt, that piece of advice is coming from a man who chased his wife for three years before she gave him a second look." The barber chuckled and shrugged.

Walt's barber added in all seriousness, "She's not all muscle and looks either. My wife had her go over our taxes from last year. We're filing an amended return. Julie says Sarah studied to be an accountant before she decided to go to that cooking school. She gave up a lot of dreams to help Julie out here in the sticks." He made eye contact with the young man who turned into a clod whenever Sarah Monroe entered a room, "My wife says that Sarah applied for a business license to do financial advising. She's going to do it part time." He added that when Jason shifted around in surprise.

Everybody quieted as Sarah left the library alone, looked for traffic and sashayed right across the street toward their guilty gazes. When she entered the barber shop with the little bell over the door chiming, her eyes swept the quieted room and smiled at Chloe who made a mad dash toward her.

Sarah raked each man's open stare and curtsied, "Gentlemen, good morning." They murmured back in near unison, and she smiled. Her eyes met Jason's, "Mr. Lambert, could Chloe come with me to the library? Annabelle and Leanne would like her to be in their craft group this morning. It lasts until eleven and maybe you could leave her with me for the day. We're getting lunch afterward and taking a little walk."

Jason nodded, "Thank you, Sarah. Chloe would you like to go?" Chloe danced beside him begging in utter joy at being saved from man talk with her father and grandfather.

Sarah held out her hand, and the little girl clasped it eagerly. Sarah's eyes danced in devilment when Walt Stone murmured, "You can take me, too." His voice dripped with the awe of seeing Sarah in broad daylight dressed up and wearing a splash of makeup. He thought she was nearly too lovely to walk down the street alone.

Sarah shook her head at Walt but took a step nearer to his chair. She looked down into his admiring eyes and winked at Chloe who was giggling. "You are such a flirt, Walt Stone. Chloe, don't you think Walt needs to get rid of those terrible sideburns?"

The little girl nodded and slid in, "They make him look like a gangster." Sarah touched the thin line of whiskers that Walt had considered his signature look since he learned to shave. He started to blush as the rest of the men chuckled.

Sarah shook her head and made a slashing touch angled from his ear toward his lips, "What do you think about there, Frank?" She made eye contact with the barber who had been trying to get the young man to shave off the ridiculous things for years. Frank nodded and squeezed Walt's shoulder when he shifted toward her, and she took a quick step back.

Sarah tugged at Chloe's hand and whispered, "Never pet a strange dog or touch a flirty man, Chloe. Bye!" she let the last word wind out in two syllables.

Walter Stone blew out his frustration with her in an expletive which made Jason laugh out loud. Walt growled to Frank, "You told her to say that didn't you? I saw you cutting Robby's hair last week and the two of you giggling over me looking in the window. Well, shave away, Frank." Walt leaned back and ignored the barber's surprise.

"I don't believe you, Walt. She was only teasing," Frank squeezed the man's shoulder again. The old man looked toward the other men in the shop, but they were busy watching Sarah prancing across the street while she talked to Chloe. Chloe was obviously reporting everything the gabby men had said because Sarah looked back toward the barbershop and waved with a grin before she went into the library. Every one of them groaned.

"I would climb a mountain to get a second look from her. It's better than wrestling alligators. Shave them off, Frank. Maybe it's time to be a bit more direct." He sat back and closed his eyes.

Later Chloe reported to her father and the rest at the dinner table that Walt had visited their picnic blanket during lunch, and he walked the town gardens and the path along the river with them later. She said that she thought Mr. Stone was the handsomest man in the whole valley who was not in her family. She told her father that Sarah had avoided Walt's efforts to kiss her when they parted, but she had agreed to take the Monroe children to movies with him in Wheeling that next weekend.

Jason examined himself in the mirror and wondered what he would do if Sarah Monroe teased him like she did Walt. He told himself that he was too old for her, too conservatively staid and far too opinionated about her lifestyle. Walt might not mind that her flirty skirts had attracted at least three men who were no longer in the picture. Jason had married a distractible woman like that. Getting Chloe out of the marriage had been the only saving grace of twelve volatile years keeping Annette under control. He wanted his next wife to be tender and malleable, not stubborn and strong like Sarah. It didn't make the thought of her bouncy, sexy walk in Lambertville any easier to forget when he saw her in the disguise of the quiet pastry chef in his kitchen on Monday morning.

CHAPTER 10

Audit

At four-thirty in the morning, the kitchen was usually a private place to set up for coffee, toss down yogurt and prepare all the dough for the day. As soon as she flicked on the lights one October morning, Sarah heard him rise from his waiting doze on the couch to confront her in the kitchen. It was not protection, but the kitchen was brightly lit. Her eyes swept him as she allowed the barrier of Maggie's station to come between them. His echoed words in Chloe's voice still hardened an edgy resistance in Sarah despite his obvious care for the children and for her the day of the fire on Lilac Hill.

Preparations were underway for another of Isabel's gatherings of old friends and important people from all over the East Coast. There were orders for gargantuan amounts of fancy plates for a tapas-style offering, so the guests could mix while sampling plates for a harvest celebration. Maggie had honed the order of expensive menu items that she wrinkled her nose considering with Lou.

Sarah thought that the appearance of Jason in the kitchen after a long absence might have to do with overtime requirements for evening. Sarah had turned down the last dinner party and finally admitted to needing a weekend in Wheeling to prepare for the CPA exam. In long, flowery letters, David Jennings was urging her to forget the whole CPA thing and come home to Boston again; his dessert team had abandoned him. He threatened to contact Jason if she didn't answer.

"Yes, Mr. Lambert? Early coffee? I haven't started baking yet. I could fill a special request," she allowed a half-smile on that last sentence because he had asked for nothing special in weeks and barely ate. Maggie had spoken to Isabel about his thinning face and worried over his new distraction with a contract he had accepted a week after the fire.

Jason nodded as if agreeing with her, "Yes. A special re-

88

quest. Sarah, do you ever feel like you are juggling everything well, and you think you can handle one more task, but it might unbalance you?"

She nodded because that was exactly how she felt since arriving in Lambertville last May. Sometimes she juggled and twirled in place with fancy tricks, and other times all the plates fell and exploded around her. She had weaned herself from the expensive medications since her move to Lilac Hill, but anxiety hovered in her periphery. Routines of regular exercise, a strict diet, work and routines with the children were the only antidotes to the worries that wanted to cripple her.

"Jennings tells me you took the CPA exam last week. Why didn't you tell me?" He sighed and put up a hand to stop a frown from completely knitting her brows, "Stop. Forget I asked that. Jennings tells me you can do an audit. I don't want to add to your stress, but I need help from someone I trust." His eyes glittered with thoughts he did not want to bubble to the surface.

Sarah leaned forward and looked at him carefully. He'd said "someone I trust," not the more obvious, "Can I trust you?" She noticed the thinning about his face and neck. The slight paunch that afflicts many men around forty was flattened. She felt red-faced to be caught looking at his belt, his chest and long arms resting on Maggie's station. The lines of his neck were taut with an odd tension.

She started hesitantly, "I audited his books. He had a sloppy bookkeeper who liked to dip in here and there." Sarah put down the towel that she'd picked up to busy herself and poured Jason a cup of coffee. She brought it to him like she had numerous times, but this time, she stayed close instead of backing up. She wanted their words to be within the space of breathing. Finances were often as closely kept as heart urges; she had learned that long ago. "You need an audit, Mr. Lambert?"

He nodded and sipped at the cup. His eyes focused on her hands clasped together and thought about the callous in each palm from shoveling the gravel, the daily work kneading, mixing and cutting, and then the intense exertion during the day of the fire. He watched her breath calmly and remembered her heaving lungs from the day she ran the exercise yard and wore out her anger with him. He had seen the field that the children referred to as "Worries Track" where she ran away and came back from the challenges of up-ending her life. A very quiet voice measured each word, "It must be done tonight. Ed Wakelin, our chief accountant, will be away without access to the accounts."

Sarah blinked in shock, "Did you arrange that?" she shook her head at the silliness of that question. She sighed, "Of course you did." She looked down and frowned deeply, "What a relief!" She hurried on because he looked so puzzled, "I worried you were sick. You've barely been eating." She smiled up at him and met the blue eyes staring back with a hunger so blatant it made her stomach ache. She couldn't tell if she was thrilled or frightened.

"It has been very tense: my mother's illness, Chloe needing extra attention, the new contract and this subtle draining of the company's reserves." He sighed and picked up one of her hands and opened it to touch one callous with his thumb, "And the worry that you might leave us. Don't leave us, Sarah." Sarah automatically raised her hand to touch his face and run her thumb over his temple which made him close his eyes. If he had been David Jennings, she might have opened her arms for a tight hug, but this was Jason Lambert who usually ended their conversations with harsh words.

Still touching his face, she asked, "What time?"

"Late this afternoon." The words allowed her to pull her hand away, "Right after his assistant leaves for the day. Could someone pick up the children?" He backed up a step as she nodded.

"I'll pay you well. Robby told me you're planning improvements to the farm. He also mentioned that Leanne might need tutoring." His eyes fell because this was where the hardness of Sarah's independence usually blistered away to insult.

Sarah nodded again and withdrew back to business, "Overtime would be good. Yes, Leanne needs sessions with a speech therapist. My plans for the kitchen and the cottage will wait."

Jason smiled and shook his head, "Current rates are $200 an hour, but I will offer a bonus based on what you save me." He shook his head again to clear it, "I'm a scientist, Sarah, not an accountant. I've been trying to check the accounts on my own every evening. Our company is built on the foundation that the government can trust us with high security contracts. If this goes public, that confidence could be lost. I've found at least $50,000 just in petty cash missing," he ruffled his hair and drank the rest of the coffee. "I think I would like pancakes this morning." He leaned forward and brushed a kiss at Sarah's temple in a surprise embrace, "Thank you, Sarah Monroe."

Sarah felt a thrill run from her temple through her body right down to her toes. She grinned up at him, "Hold on there, Mr. Lambert. One very serious demand," her eyes danced. The quiet confidence that he'd noticed in her walk last weekend was back. He expected to have to lure her with promises of a day off, spa day like his secretary always wanted or a trip somewhere exotic like his best assistant. He inclined his head and cocked an eyebrow as she said it, "Robby, Leanne and Annabelle do not eat processed foods anymore. No chips, cookies, hot dogs or soda—last time they were here, they were indulged."

Jason burst out with a laugh that was infectious. Sarah grinned though she was serious, "Miss Monroe, I expected you to ask for diamonds and chocolates. Are they being punished?"

Sarah stepped forward and shook her head smiling, "No, they are being healed. Robby has attention deficit disorder, and if Annabelle isn't hyperactive, I can't bake a tart!" She swallowed at the inkling of disapproval in his look, "I am trying diet and strict order in the house before Julie and I give up and resort to pills and therapy."

Jason nodded, "I've read the reports on that study. Perhaps you are a scientist just like me, Sarah. You have made more than fair demands; I'll warn the playroom staff." He nearly bowed before he left her.

Sarah made his pancakes and sprinkled the edges with confectioner's sugar and fresh fruit. He was on the phone when she brought the tray into the study, but his eyes followed every move as she set up the dining table and poured him a coffee. Hunger burned right through every movement that day.

By the time Sarah opened the accounts from Ed Wakelin's desk that afternoon, she felt the hollow drumming of the earth from August pounding through her body. She looked at the pictures of Wakelin's wife and children on his desktop and felt a bit irritated with him. If he had stolen from Lambert Research, he had taken something from each of the pretty people in the pictures. There was a certain dignity to sleeping blameless and innocent that they would never get back if he had stolen from the Lamberts.

After two hours, Sarah stood and stretched at the desk. She had a grasp of the ebb and flow of the business with its rich contracts, odd orders for supplies that baffled her, usual expenses like payroll, entertaining clients and advertising. Charitable deductions looked deep, but they cross-referenced without any glaring discrepancies. When Jason Lambert slipped into the office from a side door, he carried a tray of iced tea and rolls. "Maggie says you haven't eaten since your usual breakfast."

Sarah patted her flat stomach and grumbled, "Yeah, I'm falling away to nothing. Mr. Lambert, why are there financial services debits? You have an in-house accountant and a staff of financial specialists. The companies credited are geographically diverse—one in Europe, another in the States, two in the Caribbean and some in the Middle East. I know the names of the Arab cities because I remember them from the newspapers before Robert Reilly was killed."

Jason's eyes flashed over the entries she touched as she said them. He mumbled, "Robby's dad was stationed in Iraq?" His eyes crosschecked through contracts he'd negotiated himself.

Sarah shook her head, "Kuwait, but it was a short time. His

copter went down in Iraq. Have you been doing business with these holding companies?" She looked worried over what she was delving into just for a moment. Her eyes flashed toward him. It appeared to her that there had been some business with governments that she didn't remember as U.S. friendly. She frowned at her lack of political awareness.

He shook his head, "No. Not at all. I worked with a few subcontractors involved with the Iraq situation, but they are based here in the U.S. I didn't even notice these when I looked." His hand shook a bit, and he shoved it in his jacket pocket.

Sarah touched the top of the screen to indicate a number, "I am three years back in August, Mr. Lambert. This is some of the activity that leads to the trickles of funds you showed me. I traced them back—beginning with those odd debits that alerted you from this year. I think the thieving started right here." She touched one small withdraw on the screen, but Sarah dampened her excitement because he looked so horrified. She had also seen this look on David Jennings' face, but the restaurant had only lost five thousand from his bookkeeper's stock market gamble. There had been no real theft and the investment had been legitimate, but it had still damaged David's confidence in all of his employees.

She typed a few commands and accessed the whole account history for one of the financial services companies in Afghanistan. The latest payments had been made last month. None were more than a few thousand dollars, but they added up to more than a million just to the one company. Sarah gulped as Maggie popped her head in the room and called Jason to make a quick appearance at dinner because his parents were holding service until he was present. He withdrew a flash drive from his pocket and said, "Make a copy of the whole thing, Sarah. Print and highlight what you've found. I think this is bigger than a skimming of funds to line one man's pockets."

Sarah felt shaky and nervous as she made the copy and then ran reports on each of the financial services companies. She noted the companies that looked legitimate because they had copies of contracts signed by Jason in attachments. Her insides quaked when she realized that the accounts she found began while no new contracts had been accepted. She wondered if those dates would correspond with the accident that killed Jason's wife and left him so badly injured. She figured that, out in the dining room pretending to entertain guests, Jason Lambert was probably thinking the same thing.

A bit later, Maggie brought Sarah a little sandwich tray with worried eyes and a report that the children were doing fine in the playroom. Sarah rubbed her eyes and jumped back into the petty cash reports that had first alarmed Jason. Over the next hour, she found steady trickles just like she had of the restaurant books to expensive resorts, restaurants she knew the Lambert family didn't frequent and spas in exotic places. This petty thieving was a fancy disguise for the deeper runnels of cash floating away to offshore accounts and other countries. She saw it fitting like a flamboyant mask over another uglier mask.

If Jason had forced the accountant to face the theft from the expense accounts, the funds trickling out at a deeper, hidden level inside the contracts might not have been discovered. Sarah looked around the rich room with a tapestry sofa, plush carpet and high windows framing a glorious sunset and saw it all as façade. The ugliness of this deceit was jarring because the culprit seemed like a polished gentleman. Ed Wakelin attended the same church service she did, drove a sedate car and lived in an ordinary house in the valley. One of his grandchildren had been out to the farm to play with Robby one afternoon.

When she was satisfied, Sarah turned off the computer and set herself to the task of gathering all the printouts into a folder with her careful notes in the margins. She felt light-headed and eager to turn over the flash drive and the folder. She wanted to take the children and drive back to Monroe Farm as fast as she could.

Jason slipped back into the office with two martinis and a truly worried look on his face. "Trouble is coming, Sarah! Give me the flash drive," he took it and slipped it into his pocket.

She had the folder ready to give him and had set the desk back up just like she'd found it that afternoon. Rounding the corner of the desk with the folder, Jason surprised her by placing the folder on the desk and picking her up to sit right on top of it. He roughly lifted the bottom of her sweater over her head and draped it around her as if it fell there.

The outside doorknob jiggled as someone placed a key in the lock, and Jason muttered, "Sorry, Sarah." He glanced back once and then leaned over her for a kiss. His hands slid under her tee shirt and pealed it back to reveal her bare midriff as his fingers teased over bare skin. His lips left her mouth and trailed down her neck. He acted like he didn't hear the door opening or the chuckle from the man standing exposed in the hall lights.

Sarah groaned with these tactics; an observer would guess that, if uninterrupted, she would be disrobed in a few more minutes, "Mr. Lambert. Sir! We have company." She struggled to control the urge to laugh as he glanced up to her from running his fingers over her back and gave her a slight grin.

He straightened abruptly, and she fell back on the desk like butter melted in relief. He muttered, "Wakelin! Thought we'd have a little privacy in here. Aren't you supposed to be gone a few days?" His voice was husky and irritated.

Ed Wakelin wavered in the doorway a moment trying to look scandalized. His eyes searched the room furtively, "Sorry. I wondered how long you were going to wait to have that particular, little girl for dessert. Goodnight, Sarah. See you at church." He closed the door gently and laughed out loud when he heard Sarah growl out a curse for him and his holier-than-thou attitude. Jason grabbed her and hushed her with a nervous laugh. If Ed hesitated in the hallway, he must be made sure they were using his office for an interlude.

Sarah struggled to sit up properly for many minutes while Jason leaned over her and played with pulling her shirt back down and smoothing back her hair. He gave her little kisses on her hands, her forehead and her temple before she growled another curse word and kissed him back. Her tongue played at his lips before his mouth opened to her curiosity. She had wanted to taste this man for months, and from his reaction, reciprocal hunger filled him. His hands moved over her back convulsively as Sarah leaned into the kiss.

"Sarah, we have to stop." His voice was rough as he straightened. Bright sparks of the forbidden portion of this embrace dawned on both of them. Sarah's eyes flashed over his face, traced the gulley in his face from the accident and let her eyes dart back up to his shocked, wide eyes. He shook his head, "This is wrong."

Sarah felt the thrill of certain sin and uttered, "Oh no, you don't." She pulled him into her grasp with hands at his neck and kissed him again, so he could not be mistaken about her intentions. When the folder crinkled under her bottom, as he shifted her closer, she groaned at her stupidity. What was she doing with this man? They had to get themselves and the folder safely out of the office, not distract each other playing at some spark that seemed more and more illicit as they angled closer together.

Sarah pulled her shirt back down again and pushed him off her, "Well, that was a nice surprise." She touched her lips with one hand and picked up the folder with the other. A small grin emerged from her because she noticed his flushed cheeks and wide pupils. She took the folder and tucked it into her pants to lie flush along her back and tossed the sweater back over her head. She picked up the tray and smirked at him, "I'll take this to the kitchen. See you in the playroom, Mr. Lambert?"

He smoothed his hair and grimaced; he had let some terrible genie out of the bottle with this woman. If he had been curious before about her, he'd be insatiable now. When they left the office, his mother was at the far end of the hall having an animated conversation with Ed Wakelin. He rubbed his whiskers as his father joined the pair. Jason went to speak to them before meeting Sarah in the playroom. In a few moments, Jason was racing up the stairs before she could get there. He felt like all the balls he'd been juggling were out of control and falling where they would.

CHAPTER 11

The Prodigal Returns

Sarah placed the tray at the sink with quivering hands and gave the folder to Maggie. She felt muddled and confused by the audit, kissing Jason Lambert and sensing some other, roving tension in the building. Something about Ed Wakelin's sly eyes on her in the hallway made her skin prickle. Maggie had been crying, and Sarah dared to hug the other woman to her and hush her. "What is wrong, Miss Maggie? Is it more than the dinner?"

But Maggie Turner would not put it into words. Maggie shook her head and whispered, "I just do not understand." Her features had fallen into wrinkles. She growled out harshly, "I expect you back here tomorrow morning by six. No matter what happens." Her look insinuated that Sarah might be tempted to take the day off which caused a thicker cloud of confusion to fall over her. "Go up to the playroom. They are waiting for you." Maggie's eyes fell, but she took the precious folder and tucked it in the pantry desk for safekeeping.

Sarah gathered up her belongings from the kitchen and ran up the back stairs to the playroom. Isabel and Jason stood in the doorway and watched the children shrieking over a stranger bent down to talk to them. Sarah grabbed Jason's hand and squeezed, "Miss Maggie has the folder for you, Mr. Lambert." She made eye contact with him and was surprised that his face was twisted with sadness, nearly grief. "What's wrong? Miss Isabel?" They were both looking at her like they'd lost something dear.

Isabel waved her hand toward the man crowded by the children, "Well, Miss Monroe, we have something for you, dear. Jason sent another detective out to Utah. Your husband has come home!"

At that, Michael Elliott pivoted around with Annabelle in his arms and grinned toward Sarah. She gasped at his razor-short hair that revealed the furrow of a healed wound at the crown of his head. He was much thinner, tanned and growing out a full, dark beard. His grin fled immediately when he recognized her. Michael and Sarah stared at each other in shock for many moments while Sarah's grasp on Jason's hand tightened.

Michael's voice was deep and gentle but far from the mellowed tones he used for her sister, "Sarah Monroe! How are you, sweetheart? What are you doing here?"

Sarah let go of Jason to cross the floor as Michael unfolded his body and stood with Annabelle sniffling into his neck. Sarah gave him a bit of a bashful hug which was much less effusive than the one she had given David Jennings, her former boss. She broke away and peered up at him, "I work for the Lamberts, Michael. I've been here about six months. What happened to you?" She looked at the healed-over gash and wondered how he'd been injured.

Both Jason and Isabel watched their meeting and glanced at each other in confusion. Jason thought in clogged, partial sentences and heard only his thumping heart. He thought that she was acting oddly and wanted to scold her again for this lukewarm reception of her long, lost husband.

Michael was excited and a bit too loud, "Sarah, I was beaten up and left for dead. I didn't even know my name for months and then some man came through town flashing a picture and asking about me. The lady I was staying with told me about him a month ago. It came back in dreams, little flashes. Sarah, tell me Julie is all right." The anguish in his voice told his fears. "How is my wife? Where is my Julie?" He held Sarah's hand and looked into her eyes like he could read truth there.

Sarah shook herself in a sudden shiver as both of the Lamberts gasped at his words. "Julie is fine. She moved here to the farm at Lilac Hill after she quit her job in Wheeling. She took an overnight job at the mine office to pay the bills; that's why the kids are with me this evening. She's there now on the 2nd shift." Sarah's eyes flashed back to Jason's confusion. Suddenly she understood that Jason had brought Michael back through some sort of force, "What did you think, Michael? Did you think she'd move away or take up with some other man?"

The bitterness made Robby tug at Sarah's hand and whine for her to stop. Sarah held herself stiffly, "Do you really want to come home to Monroe Farm, Michael? Julie wondered if you chose to stay away."

Michael frowned, "Of course, I want to come home. I wouldn't have come with Lambert's man if I hadn't. I do love Julie and the kids. I'm not saying it isn't hard sometimes. We fight and she is. . ." he ran out of words looking at Robby and Leanne who'd been there and witnessed the arguments. He sighed deeply, "Sarah, sometimes your sister is a regular mess." He looked down at her face with a grave look.

Sarah frowned at that thought, "Yes, Michael, she is. You left a severely depressed woman with three little children and disappeared off the face of the earth. What were you thinking? Why didn't you come home? I've seen the activity on your checking account. I saw the long distance bill. You hadn't called for weeks before your truck was found. You drained the checking account and turned the tags in on the truck." A bit of the anger she'd thrown away caught up with her suddenly. She thought of Julie and the children as she'd found them in May with dulled, lifeless eyes existing in the filthy house. A disaster had been narrowly avoided. Only with all those months of distance and struggle was she allowed to see it.

Leanne ended it suddenly by clinging to Michael and insisting, "Sarah, please don't make him go away like you did with my daddy. My daddy was a bad, mean man who hurt us, but Michael is good all the way through like an angel." She tugged at Michael, "Michael, we help out now. Sarah cleaned the house and gave us all jobs. Mommy doesn't cry as much anymore."

Isabel was sobbing in Jason's arms and made Sarah choke back further anger. Jason had that crumpled look that he'd worn months ago when Sarah had the panic attack in the kitchen. His face had become red and mottled.

Sarah's eyes filled with tears, but she resisted letting it go,

"You could have called me, Michael. You could have told me she was depressed, and you couldn't handle it. She was doing better than you'd expect. She was working. Your friend Walt and his parents helped her."

Michael lurched forward and grabbed at Sarah forcing her into his chest. His arms clamped like steel around her back. He shook her a little for some sense, "Sarah, you tell me she was taking care of the kids. I bet you had to wade through trash to find the kitchen. I bet they hadn't any clean clothes or food to eat." She didn't answer as she held herself stiff in his arms. "What did she do? Call you crying and ruin college for you again? What did you leave behind this time for her, Sarah? A chance to finish your degree? A good job? A man you loved? Shit, girl, I appreciate the effort, but you don't have to sacrifice your life for Julie."

Sarah struggled away from him and whispered with barely controlled anger making her voice rasp, "Yes, I do, Michael. I love these children, and if you two can't handle it this time, you give them to me. I want them. Yes, I have changed my whole life, and I would do it over and over again. Do you hear me, Michael Elliott? Do you know why?" Anger had replaced the anguished panic she usually felt if her emotions ran away.

Michael nodded, "Because that's who you are, Sarah Monroe." They glared at each other for a few more minutes until both their shoulders fell in exhaustion. Jason was confused and silent trying to figure out the twists and turns of their volatile relationship.

Then Robby made Michael smile and allowed his shoulders to fall from the fighter's tension Sarah caused. Robby put his two cents in, "Wait till you see the house, Mike. We planted a garden, painted every room and unpacked all the boxes. Sarah makes us clean up, and we help keep it in order just like Leanne said. Now we go to church every week, the Lutheran one because Sarah says it's what people do to belong. We are eating vegetables right out of the garden we grew this year!" Leanne quietly added that she was learning to read and that her best friend in the world was Chloe Lambert. Sarah began to cry as if all the tension from May had been dammed up in her too long.

Michael extended a hand to Jason Lambert who took it in utter shock, "Thank you for sending that man to speak to me, Mr. Lambert. I thought I'd been gone too long to come back. When I woke up in the hospital in Utah, I had no ID or money. When I did remember, it was too easy just to stay away than to deal with being me. Thank you for bringing me home." Jason shook Michael's hand and realized how young a man he was to shoulder so much responsibility.

In a flash, Jason thought about the same weight that had been balanced by Sarah for months though none of it was of her making. He had been so harsh and judgmental with her because he assumed Robby, Leanne and Annabelle were her children, not her sister's. His mind overbalanced with the confusion of Michael's words, the treachery of Ed Wakelin and Sarah's harsh strength. The noise from the children all speaking at the same time washed over him.

When his father stepped into the room, Joseph Lambert signaled to his son that he was needed. Jason figured that the government agents he called before dinner had arrived. His father had waylaid Ed with a bogus discussion on international trade agreements. Jason nodded to his father and left Michael Elliott with one thought, "Michael, I still don't remember much of the months after my accident, and it was three years ago. Give yourself time. Learn to forgive yourself."

He turned and left the room as Sarah gathered up the children and fled the mansion. The events of the day were spinning by her so fast; she knew she needed to retrieve her sister and get back to the safety of Monroe Farm. She needed one long run on Worries Track.

When Sarah arrived the next morning at five, Maggie gave her a hard look and gestured to the menu posted on the corkboard with assignments. Some fearsome anger worked the old woman's jaw. Sarah remembered Maggie's tears last night. Sarah quieted her questions because she understood the distance needed to work out problems. Sarah had no sooner finished an unusually large pastry order when Maggie tapped on an order for bread.

During the thinking time supplied while the kneading of the dough, Sarah decided that she had done something to cause the gaff between them and began to revisit every conversation for the last week that included Maggie. She set the loaves to rise in their dusty little pans by eight and stretched her back. She had surprised a snake on the track that morning and had wrenched a muscle skidding to a stop. The snake had slipped away unharmed, but the pain in her back had grown stiff.

Out of the corner of her eye, she watched Maggie bore holes into her work. Sarah shook her head and whirled around, and said "Uncle!" At Maggie's surprised look, she continued, "What have I done wrong? I will grovel, plead, take the kitchen, so you have a day off, but please stop looking at me like I've done something evil." Since Sarah never spoke much, the stream of words made Maggie smile.

"There's my girl. Have you been honest with me in all things?" Maggie nodded just like Sarah did with an open-mouthed, shocked look. Maggie slammed her pounding mallet on an unoffending cutlet. She shook her head, "Do you even realize that the Lamberts thought those three, little children were yours from shacking up with assorted boyfriends? Jason had you investigated, and you've never been married. I guess he didn't think to look up birth certificates for the children—too personal and not Jason's style." She shook her head, "We are all so embarrassed! What terrible things he said to you!"

"Oh Lord!" Sarah felt giddy, as all the tension blew away leaving her exposed and somehow free of confusion for the first moment in months. "Why would anyone think that? I'm just a duffer in the mother department, Miss Maggie. I feel like every mistake I made with them was recorded and commented on by Jason Lambert! Overbearing man!" Her brows furrowed as each of their conversations colored by that mistaken assumption further muddled his intentions.

"I was just seventeen when Robby was born. My goodness, Miss Maggie! No wonder he thought I should loosen up and go for a roll in the hay with Walt last summer! Chauvinist!" She thought through her efforts to take the children to church, community events and the library to entertain them and give them a sense of community. He had been trying to be kind to a very immature and seemingly careless, promiscuous girl. Sarah groaned as her cheeks flared a ruddy shade, "With all of Julie's escapades, I've never even had a serious boyfriend!" Sarah shook her head and pointed out the door, "You get the walk in the garden today, Miss Maggie. It's time for me to prepare the main dish."

Maggie nodded and left Sarah to prepare the most tender pork dish the Lamberts had ever served guests at lunch. Sarah thought about every conversation, every condescending comment and relived Jason Lambert's kisses half a dozen times as she made lunch and plated it. She considered poisoning his lunch or at minimum giving him a painful stomachache. She reminded herself that he was grappling with the theft of company funds by Wakelin which was fuel for a bit of forgiveness.

When two FBI agents came in to fetch her for an interview, the lead investigator complimented her gravely, "I have never met a CPA who could cook anything but books. The luncheon was a real pleasure, Miss Monroe." As they left the kitchen, Billy and Lou smiled as they heard the man try to get her herbed red potatoe recipe for his wife.

When the afternoon staff met with the morning crew, Sarah had angrily announced that she was no unwed mother or serial monogamist. Her delivery made them all laugh. Lou told her he had an unmarried brother in Charleston and winked. Billy patted her on the back, "I thought it was weird that a serious, young guy like Walt Stone would be so hot for you if you were married to his friend from Wheeling. Sweetie, I knew something was mixed up the night of the fire when I met your sister, but we were all so excited with the ridge burning, I didn't pay attention. I take it your sister is married to that Elliott boy from Wheeling?" Sarah nodded and shook her head ruefully. What had they thought of her? Would they think that she could abandon her children to go off to college for a few years? How heartless and cruel.

Ed Wakelin was led away in handcuffs, and by three, all the firm's records were seized and every holding overseas and domestic was frozen. Jason sat at the dining room table with his father and brother reviewing records and sorting out contracts. Sarah worked with the rest of Lambert Research's executive staff, the FBI, and its auditors for ten hours straight to untangle the accounts and leave Jason with a scaled-down business to support his family and employees.

When the all clear was given to restricted access to current accounts, everyone started to feel relieved. The FBI had agreed to turn the investigation over to a task force for a possible international fraud ring but not to expose Jason's company to bankruptcy or unwanted publicity. The staff looked drained and exhausted after the cutting and dividing of assets resulted in a new company that would leave Jason a smaller research company but a completely solvent one. It was two in the morning before anyone stood up to leave Wakelin's office now littered with coffee cups and plates.

Sarah sat stiffly and kneaded her back from the wrenching early the previous morning. Wandering back to the kitchen with a tray of debris from the team, she ran a hand over her station, walked down the hallway and stared at the car. She knew she wasn't fit to drive the fifteen minutes home. It was the first day she hadn't worried over the children for nearly six months, and it left her feeling empty.

She decided to crash on the couch in the playroom to escape the phone calls to clients, paperwork assembled to apply for a new business license and investigators talking all at the same time. The drone in the dining room and Jason's study was like a construction site of words and questions. She found an old throw blanket, slipped off her shoes and placed a small pillow under her knees before she stretched out like a corpse. Exhaustion flooded her vision behind dry eyelids with little blue arcs of pain, but her body gave up and threw her into deep sleep.

Sarah dreamed she was dancing with a solid, warm man who had a firm grip. She looked up to see with whom she was clutched tight as the music swelled, and Sarah met her father's eyes. She continued the dance through to the next song and hung onto his thoughts. "You are such a smart little girl; you'll figure it out." He frowned, "Race with yourself, Sarah. Don't let anyone else set the pace." And then with a warm smile, "I know she's older, but you look out for Julie." He began to fade thinking, "I love you, baby. Never forget how I love you." John Monroe looked like the tall, blond-haired man who smiled down at her mother in their wedding portrait. His voice was the soothing one he'd used to ease Sarah into sleep after childhood nightmares.

She tried to send her thoughts back to him, but she was trapped in that silence she'd used on Jason Lambert for months, so he'd leave her alone. Breaking through the silence forced her eyes open. She was alone in the playroom of the Lambert's fine mansion. She lay there for many minutes reliving the last few days, replaying the dream of her father and considering the future near and far.

She heard activity downstairs from many workers, perhaps a gathering in the great dining room that could open to the sunroom for dancing. She dragged a hand through her hair, checked that her clothes weren't too creased and crept down the back stairs in bare feet and stood in the back of a crowded room. Sarah slid into a group of gardeners and grounds men she knew from wandering the property and fighting the fire on Lilac Hill.

Jason, his father Joseph and his brother Stephen were standing before the staff of the great house and research firm. They were flanked by the investigators who had first spoken to Sarah. Stephen was explaining the theft of over three million dollars in expense money that drained the firm. He added, "The culprit has been arrested. There will be no layoffs. The firm and our family need every employee now more than ever." A general sigh of relief swept the room.

Joseph stepped forward, "We are asking for patience with changes in the next few weeks. There may be media attention and some might offer lucrative deals to share information on the company." He gave everyone a sad smile. Sarah felt as though he was speaking directly to her, "I want to remind you that we treat this staff like family. We trust you in the same way." He asked that anyone who felt uncomfortable with restricting free speech to the press could see him privately.

Then Jason took Isabel's hand as she sat right in front of him. He thanked the staff for their dedication and promised to fulfill each of the outstanding contracts signed by Lambert Research. He announced, "The trading name for the company has been changed to 'Lilac Hill Research.' Again, there will be no layoffs or closures due to the investigation of Ed Wakelin." The room was rocked by tumultuous applause as the staff understood that the Lamberts had saved their jobs in the rural area where few existed. The news of the changes brought out calls for silly toasting, and even the FBI men smiled.

Sarah stepped back into the hallway and padded into the kitchen. She slipped back on her shoes and glanced at the clock shocked that it was one o'clock. She began the bread for the evening meal without any thought of going to see Jason. After all, when he wanted her, he would know where to look.

CHAPTER 12

Lavender Cottage

During the week after the upheaval on Lilac Hill, Chloe's birthday cake became an endeavor for Sarah alone. After spending an afternoon in the kitchen complaining about boring cakes, Chloe decided to design a multilayered cake with assorted flavors ribboning between each thin layer. Maggie thought it sounded like a disaster, but Sarah laughed and said that the four-year-old should get her wish. Cake design provided a pleasant distraction from bookkeeping, reunions and other tensions.

Jason hadn't spoken to Sarah alone for over a week, but she chose not to take it to heart. What she took to heart was the thought that all that breathless kissing and touching happened at the precipice of great change for him and while her supposed husband was on his way home. If Jason was going to declare any serious interest in her, he had chosen a very odd time to do it. If Michael had been her missing husband, she reasoned as she ran the track after looking out for snakes and other scary creatures, all Jason had managed to do was muddy the waters. She concluded that her internal, churning waters were as dense as Billy's gravy.

So Sarah worked each day in a companionable silence and taught Chloe a few tricks with cake decorating. She noticed that Maggie acted wary with her and that the elder Lamberts stayed cloistered in their residence at the mansion.

At home on Lilac Hill, Michael and Julie readjusted to their new life together. They seemed to love each other more than they had on their wedding day, but they also argued more fiercely. Michael's friends trickled to the house for beers on the porch, impromptu dinners and evenings of storytelling. Sarah felt invaded by the clutter of men and irritated by the extra noise that disrupted the children's evening routine.

When Sarah opened the family account book at the end of the week to pay their bills, Michael stood over her shoulder and offered advice. He added when Sarah glared back at him, "I can't go back to driving until I'm released by a doctor. I'll call the trucking company and make it right."

Sarah narrowed her eyes at such promises. She had been through promises from Leanne's father in the past. She had assembled a few too many financial statements for other people barely hanging on to take his words at face value. She tried to be calm, "You had my sister cosign that loan. Whatever you do, don't default on it. They will foreclose on this house."

"You have no right . . . Julie and I are partners," Michael clenched his fists trying to control his anger.

Sarah stood to look up into Michael's red face, "And she owns half this farm with me. You default and we all fail, Michael." She took a step toward him with two fingers poised as if holding a sliver of dough, "We are this close to bankruptcy. If you want to help, get a job." She waited for him to flare at her, but his shoulders fell.

He nodded, "I know, Sarah. I know what I have to do." He unclenched his fists and stepped back, "Both your boss Lambert and my buddy Walt have said the same thing." He let out a breath in a gust, "Why is it harder to hear you say it?"

Sarah felt something click inside; this man was as mild as her sister was gentle. He was no violent man like Thompson, a supposing creature like Jason or a kind tyrant like David Jennings. She shrugged, "I'm the little sister? You didn't marry me, and yet, here we are living in each other's way." Sarah let herself smile at Michael. At that moment, she considered him a moody adolescent.

Michael nodded and put up both hands, "Okay, truce."

The often repeated, barely believable tale that Michael made of his disappearance irritated Sarah. Walt caught her rolling her eyes one evening, pursed his lips and shook his head at her. She slipped out the door to escape the antic laughter filling the house. Walt followed her out onto the porch where she stood wrapped in a light sweater and glaring at the emerging stars. His soft-spoken, deep voice chided her, "He's trying to make sense of it, Sarah. I hear the story changing, too, but Julie is happy to have him back."

Sarah nodded and tried to let her shoulders loosen, "I know, Walt. I understand it in my head, but the children were at risk the whole time, and both of them are still so self-absorbed. I know you tried to help."

She saw him bite back a denial. He sighed, "Michael told me what you said about taking custody if they can't handle the kids. I need to tell you—Julie called you because I threatened to do the same or call Social Services. It was even worse than what you walked into last May."

Sarah felt the buffet of his worries in his low voice. She turned toward him and offered, "I'm so glad you were here."

"Sweetheart, I am so glad you came home when you did."

They stood on the dark porch side-by-side until they were called back inside by Leanne asking for a bedtime story and by Robby with a question for Walt Stone. When Sarah looked in on Annabelle while the little girl slept, Sarah saw that the stones from the gravel-spreading day were arranged in family groups with comical faces dotting them. Sarah touched Annabelle's hair and noticed for the first time that it had lost its toddler downy softness.

When the older Monroe cousins visited with Michael's parents one weekend, Sarah made the excuse of an appointment and spent the day with Nancy Ann Stone. They walked around a farmer's market and craft fair. They examined produce and discussed recipes like girlfriends. Nancy Ann squeezed Sarah's hand when Walt and his father joined them for lunch after reviewing the tractor and truck display. Walt's mother whispered, "He's way too serious most of the time, honey. It's cute how he gets all clumsy around you." Sarah let that thought take a seat in her mind right along with all of the other worries, but she enjoyed the day away from the Elliott homecoming.

Michael stood over Sarah one morning when the alarm rang at four and asked her if it was necessary. "I don' need to get up until six to get Robby and Leanne ready for school, and the alarm really puts my teeth on edge."

Sarah sleepily grumbled at him, "I wonder if spending all that money on a private detective was worth it." She flipped off the alarm and turned over to dismiss him. The old bed frame squeaked and reminded her of her temporary fit in their nuclear family.

Later he came behind her and hugged her as she stood looking out on the dark fields. Michael apologized, "I'm sorry for being a grouch, darling."

Sarah started thinking about staying but leaving at the same time. Walt lived right in Lambertville not ten minutes from his parents. He spent time with them, but they weren't in each other's way. She understood why Jason and his family had assumed she was the children's mother; they treated her that way. She had established her rule over their lives, and though she offered order and security, the Elliotts were a more relaxed family. Three parents, even in a large house, felt like one too many.

The afternoon of Chloe's birthday party, Sarah gave the little girl her gift during the quiet of the one o'clock break. Sarah felt reticent about the invitation to the party because she knew that Julie was bringing Leanne and Annabelle. After Sarah's hard words about depression were repeated to Julie by Michael, her sister gave Sarah a wide berth at times and forcefully took a more active part with the children. Sarah's offer to take the children if their parents couldn't handle it, shook them.

The evening of Chloe's party, Robby and Michael were headed back into town for soccer practice that would have been impossible before Michael's return. If Sarah went home directly after work, she would be alone on the farm for the first time that fall, and she would not be the interloper on Chloe's party attended by family and a few friends.

So during the one o'clock break, Sarah gave Chloe a little recipe book that she had filled with all the recipes she'd taught the little girl, the cookies they'd made for Chloe's tea party, and her favorite dishes from the rest of the staff. There was room to add pages as her repertoire increased. Chloe hugged Sarah and whispered, "You are the mother I dream about, Miss Sarah. Do you dream about your parents?"

Sarah had been taken aback by her words, "Yes, Chloe, I just dreamt about my father. We were dancing, and he was giving me advice." She smoothed back the little girl's hair like she'd wanted to months ago. Her heart weighed heavy and tender under her breastbone.

Chloe held out the book and opened it to a blank page and printed something neatly, "Write down his advice so I can follow it." The page was titled, "Recipe for Life."

Sarah nodded and printed, "Race with yourself. Don't let anyone else set the pace." She added the name "John Robert Monroe" beneath the words. Sarah told Chloe that she would be trying to follow that advice today and wouldn't stay for the party. Chloe nodded sagely and skipped back to the playroom.

Sarah found the keys to the old caretaker's cottage in the kitchen drawer where they'd deposited them four years ago when they opened the farmhouse in the twilight of their first night. It had been the early spring of the year their father had died. Sarah had come home because John Monroe had called to say that Julie was moving back with him. He'd been the one to say, "Things are bad, Sarah." His voice had warned her with her name uttered in two low notes.

He would die a few months later during a rare meal where they were gathered to spend a Sunday afternoon huddled in the house. Julie had just received the divorce decree, and John Monroe had insisted she stay away from her ex-husband who'd become violent. John Monroe had looked at his girls and fumbled with the pen he'd been using to point out details in the agreement, "Sarah, you must help your sister. Communication is the key."

Sarah had been nodding absently as she cleared the dishes from the table. He fell forward onto the table and then slid sideways. Dishes Sarah had not gathered clattered to the floor as the tablecloth pulled with his slumping body. Though Sarah tried resuscitation while Julie sobbed into the phone, their father was dead.

Sarah would often cry until she slept that year in her old Trenton bedroom. She took a job waiting tables, so Julie could keep her job at the bank. Julie had been promoted to head teller despite giving birth to Leanne and missing time from work to meet with the lawyer and appear in court. Julie had even bailed Mark Thompson out of jail after sending him there a number of times. Sarah offered support, tried to help out with Robby and Leanne and learned how to make pies from the diner's head cook. After they sold the house in Trenton and stayed for one sweet summer at Lilac Hill, Sarah had returned to Boston wanting to study more than accounting. Cooking and baking kept her mind from wandering too far into sorrow. One evening course at the community college led to serious study at the academy and an internship at Majorane.

Sarah held the keys to the cottage until they warmed in her palm and looked around the main house noting the changes she'd made to the order and cleanliness of it since she arrived. Suddenly she had that Poppins urge to pack up and leave because her work was done. She considered the siren's call of Boston and Chef Jennings. She hesitated over thoughts of flirty Walt Stone and his parents, stalwart Miss Maggie, her new friends Lou and Billy, the complicated Jason Lambert and the children. The thought of the children stopped her from leaving because she knew she wanted to witness more than a few months of their lives. She didn't want to be the favorite aunt who sent big gifts from the city. She wanted to be Sarah whom they could depend on for fierce protection and constancy.

She looked out the kitchen door toward the old cottage. How badly deteriorated could it be if there had been a caretaker living there when they visited as children? Sarah was curious and itchy enough with discomfort in her room at the farmhouse to find out if the cottage was habitable. She waded through the taller grass that they hadn't bothered to cut fifty yards beyond the porch. The old path between the houses was obscured with dried grasses and dirt.

The cottage had a narrow porch covered by the extended roof and two windows framing a single door. The peeling paint on the door had scattered onto the porch boards, but the four panes of old, wavy glass in it were unmarred. The key turned, and the door swung open without any effort. Sarah entered with a flashlight and stepped carefully inside, half-expecting to fall through the floorboards. She smiled grimly thinking about her foolhardy approach to everything last spring with the children. She found the breaker box in the kitchen and threw the main switch for the electric. She listened for any snapping or crackling of frayed wires. The wind outside was the only sound along with her careful breathing.

Dust was thick on every surface, but whoever had lived there kept a neat, well-ordered house. Sarah toured each of the rooms hardly daring to move a thing. The four rooms on the first floor had little furniture or personal belongings.

The kitchen was a tight galley that opened to a small dining area with an oiled, rough-hewn table. The table was the first surface that Sarah cleaned. She examined the stove and decided it was rusty and dangerous, but she had lived off of a hot plate and a microwave most of the years she'd lived in Boston. She shrugged and searched until she found the water lines and twisted the valve to open the cold line. The pipes thrummed when she ran water into the sink, and she jumped when a well pump whirred into action. The water ran nearly clear after a few moments of brown then rusted orange that quickly shifted to a pale amber flow. She opened a cabinet and found a jelly jar like it had been left there for her. She let the water run for a few minutes and took a sample just like they'd done four years ago at the main house to have it tested at the hardware store.

Rubbing her cold hands down her legs as twilight descended, Sarah experimented with a few lights in each room so that soon, the whole place was lit. Upstairs there were two bedrooms: one was cozy and faced the burned-out edges of the forest on Lilac Hill, and the other was big enough to accommodate a larger bed and looked toward the farmhouse. The single bathroom was long and narrow to accommodate a claw-foot tub like the one at the main house and an oversized, rusty porcelain-glazed sink. "You'll do," she muttered.

A towering, walnut-colored wardrobe in the hallway contained aged clothing. She giggled in nervousness as she pulled the glass knob to peek inside. The cabinet was large enough to step into like one in the old children's novel and had enough room for three of Sarah's spare versions of both summer and winter wardrobes. Sarah examined the contents and withdrew a long dress and held it up to herself in the long, mirrored door. The gown was a luxurious, pale green satin and had the ivory gloves draped over another smaller hanger at the back. The color of the gown complimented her dark hair and highlighted her china-blue eyes.

The girl that looked back at Sarah in the wardrobe mirror had become a stern-looking woman who was in charge of herself. Sarah looked closer at her eyes that seemed a darker, richer blue in the half-light and then at the sprinkle of freckles under clear skin tanned from the relentless walking and running every day. Her cheekbones had emerged from previous baby fat and comfortable living. Her hair was longer; highlighted gold streaks contrasted the deep brown underneath.

She lowered the dress and looked at her neck and chest. In this slender form, she had become an attractive woman quite unlike her voluptuously beautiful sister with her sky-blue eyes and honey-blond hair. They had been bound together for the past seven years, so that Sarah had forgotten she was a separate person who did not have to love the men her sister did. She wondered when she adopted Julie's life as her own, and remembered the weight of love they'd both felt for Robert Reilly. Her memories of school and running the neighborhood with Julie were enmeshed with Robert's presence as neighbor, friend and adopted big brother. His loss still rested in a burn at the back of her throat. Sarah had grown to hate Mark Thompson, and probably like her sister, did not have complete faith in Michael Elliott's prostrations of love and fidelity.

Her eyes moistened. Sarah missed acting as a mother to Robby, Leanne and Annabelle. Doing that for even a few months had challenged her to grow into this person who looked back at her. She examined at her calloused hands and remembered Jason Lambert's touch. He had been tender with the parts of her that showed she was willing to learn to live in this place.

She let the tears run down because the woman in the mirror was a fine cook, a wizard with pastry dough and fancy cakes, but no soft woman who could partner a Lambert. If Jason had wanted her, he wanted the excitement of some other man's woman. Worse yet, he had been intrigued with a woman who would collect children like souvenirs from old lovers and then leave them behind.

She replaced the pretty dress and wondered about the woman who left the clothes in the wardrobe. Had she intended to return? The woman would have been about her height and weight, and the clothes were made of fine fabric. Sarah felt through the closet and found four sets of men's clothes and one formal Sunday suit, a black felt hat and a few pairs of shoes.

In the back corner of the wardrobe leaned a polished .38 rifle wrapped up in a flannel lap blanket. She remembered learning to shoot a gun like it at this farm. She tried to remember the gun she held last when she was ten and wondered if it was the same one. There was a box of cartridges in the very bottom of the closet, but nothing in the gun itself.

She heard Michael's truck roar into the yard and hesitate as it sputtered and died in front of the house. Everything they owned was chugging along on its last legs. Sarah walked back through the house turning off lights. As a caution, she picked up the flashlight and flipped the main breaker to extinguish the power for the night. If Jason Lambert paid her overtime for the audit, she might be able to afford an hour for an electrician and another for a plumber to look over the place before she committed to buying a bed. She suddenly wanted her own bed, a new bed that she might lure a lover to someday. She was tired of the creaking frame of her narrow bed from Trenton. Sarah Monroe picked up her flashlight and guided herself carefully back to the farmhouse on Lilac Hill.

Michael was a good source of capable friends in the area who had home improvement expertise. When Sarah explained her plan for the cottage, she was surprised that Michael didn't move her there that evening. Julie returned to the farm irritated with her husband's eagerness to rid them of Sarah's presence and Sarah's disappearing act that afternoon. Hands on hips as she read Michael and Sarah's list of needs for the cottage, Julie tried to scold Sarah, "I don't want you living alone. Even as close as the cottage, you are escaping again. And Sarah, when you decide not to go places like that party today, you have to let someone know."

Sarah had glanced up at her sister and shrugged, "I told Chloe. It was her party."

Julie gave her sister a long look, "You told a four-year-old! When you didn't answer the phone here, I thought Jason Lambert was going to send someone out to check on you. What are you avoiding, Sarah?"

Sarah just shook her head and glanced at Michael's grin. He teased her, "You didn't tell your sister about you and Jason Lambert did you? Julie, Lambert thought the kids belonged to Sarah. He thought he was returning Sarah's husband when he sent that detective out there to talk to me." He looked softly at Sarah, "There were so many sparks flying between the two of you the night they brought me back, I expected Lambert to declare himself right on the spot." He grinned at both of them in obvious enjoyment of Sarah's embarrassment.

Julie shook her head, "So you have managed to get involved with the boss! I noticed all those looks the night of the fire. Sarah, of all people, I would have expected you to avoid that mess," she smiled and thought about the man she'd met twice and her little sister. "I still think he's odd, but he does seem concerned about you, Sarah. Tonight he relaxed after his little girl showed him your gift and Dad's advice. She told him you were busy racing at your own pace. I don't think she really understood it, but he seemed to get it."

Sarah rolled her eyes at her sister and brother-in-law. She felt more comfortable now that she'd figured out how to give them privacy and had avoided Chloe Lambert's party. Sarah's little bubble of distance was intact, porous but firm like a fine sponge cake.

CHAPTER 13

Late Autumn Chill

Of all people, Michael called Walt Stone to come out the next day and look over Sarah's cottage. Walt had apprenticed with his electrician uncle before taking a liquor distributor's job in Wheeling. That driving job had opened the door to buying the route as an independent business a few years later. It allowed the man to live near his parents in Lambertville, keep up with all of his old buddies like Michael, and drive up and down the main highway for work.

Walt spent about an hour inspecting the little cottage before she arrived home from work the day after Chloe's party. Walt and Sarah talked at the main house with Michael before she gathered some cleaning supplies and returned with him to the cottage. He warned Sarah about aluminum wiring which the cottage was so old it didn't have and replaced a few switches he thought were corroded. He glanced at the ancient furnace and suggested a heat pump like he'd just installed at his parent's house. Sarah rolled her eyes at the suggestion and told him she wasn't a millionaire.

They walked through every room in the house and made a list of repairs and improvements that would make the cottage habitable. Walt stood behind her seated form and suggested items. He stepped closer a number of times to jab at an item, but his eyes were focused on her neck, her cleavage, and her mouth. He wanted her mouth soft on his and her lips opening. It was no wonder he felt clumsy and inept as he stood behind her and ached to touch her.

Walt tried to be a gentleman the entire visit, but insisted on a kiss as she paid him their agreed upon fee. He actually smiled when she stepped away from him. He ran a hand through his hair looking at her, "Sarah, you can't blame me for trying. You are one beautiful woman, and I'd like to take you out."

Sarah walked him to the door of the cottage with a bemused smile. She was tempted because the man without his loud drinking buddies was quiet and soft-voiced. She liked him better after watching him have a good time with the children and his parents on the canning day. The night they went to the movies, he only tried to kiss her once and took her arm like a gentleman while they walked. He certainly backed off when she resisted the kiss despite the fact that she was quite defenseless alone with him. She looked at him eye-to-eye as he turned back half way down the front steps. He was handsome in the rough-cheeked, working man way. Without the hat and the swagger of town dance bravado, there was something comfortable about the man. Sarah examined his thick, brown hair like hers, large brown eyes and the likeable face especially when he grinned through his embarrassment of being rejected again. She softened her heart just a touch.

He hesitated and glanced at his truck parked in front of the main house before turning toward her once more, "It doesn't have to be strictly romantic, Sarah. I would like to spend some time getting to know you." She smiled at his candid, plain invitation and agreed to go dancing on Saturday night. She made it clear that she did not want fancy dinner, hadn't been drinking for quite some time and valued her good reputation in the small town. He tipped his hat to her and said, "Yes, Sarah." The poor man fantasized about a big bed in the little bedroom at Lilac Hill all the rest of that week.

Sarah hummed to herself as she cooked at the Lamberts' kitchen after she moved into the cottage she dubbed "Lavender Cottage" though the children called it "Sarah's House." There were little blueprints of the house in every sketch she doodled. Billy was keeping an eye out for a stove after she invited him out late the first week to look over the plumbing and the furnace. He and Lou agreed that no self-respecting cook ate off a hot plate at home. She laughed and said, "You have no idea what I put up with living in Boston on a shoestring." Billy drove into town with her and ran up an extraordinary bill one Saturday on paint, plumbing supplies and a ceiling fan he was sure Walt could put up in the kitchen. Sarah scraped the bottom of her savings and bought another for the main bedroom thinking about the heat of the previous summer.

She cleaned the cottage top to bottom in the first week and painted it in the next week. When Walt Stone took her out for their second date, he teased her about the bluish-lavender paint she hadn't quite removed from under her fingernails. When she stood in better light inside the tavern as a touring country band turned the place into a dance hall, the black lights revealed that Sarah was marked here and there with paint she hadn't noticed.

Dabbing one finger in his mouth, Walt tried to rub off a dot of paint on the back of her arm. She smiled at him and rubbed off the places left from painting all the trim on the porch and the front door with the pale color a shade deeper than periwinkle blue. Jason Lambert caught his eye once while Walter was attending to peeling off the offensive paint off her arm while she laughed at one of his friends acting silly.

Walt used any excuse he could to touch her and lay some claim to this woman who seemed even more removed than last summer. Walt held her as close as she let him and looked up to focus on his glib conversation as they danced, but he felt her having another internal debate in her head.

Whenever he looked toward the bar, Jason Lambert was there staring at them. That night his hair stood up on his neck considering the scarred man's constant observation, so he asked Sarah if she'd like an ice cream. It was cold and brisk outside, but that night she agreed with a puzzle on her face. The weekend before, they had danced most of the evening, and he had been satisfied with gentle kisses on her porch when he delivered her back to the cottage.

They grabbed their coats, said a few good nights and left the heat of the bar to walk along the few blocks that made up the town of Lambertville. Sarah held his arm and looked in the windows of the stores they passed. She slowed as they passed a furniture store. "Are you buying a bed for your house soon? Michael says you're being thick-headed about taking your bed from the main house." Walt was diving at something to say to this unfathomable woman.

She looked up to wink at him, "I have to save a few hundred more because I want the best mattress they sell. I have put up with the worst beds my entire life. Sleeping on that old divan in the living room is nothing next to the dorm rooms. That bed in the main house is the one I've slept in since I left the crib; it should be thrown away. A good bed and a decent kitchen under a roof that doesn't leak: that is my definition of home."

Walt nodded, "And the right man in that bed, Sarah. Sweetheart, I want to be honest. I'd like to take you home and get you into my bed, a nice, big expensive bed by the way, but it's not what you want." He kissed her on the cheek and hugged her to his chest. Walt caught the reflection of the two of them in this embrace in the furniture store window. It was a shame because they did suit each other in height and slender, dark looks.

Sarah didn't know what to say to Walt Stone who had been nothing but a gentleman. She felt angry with herself for being so transparent. "I'm sorry, Walt. I do like you, you know."

Walt shook his head and grinned at her crestfallen face, "I'm glad you do. Well, I hope that Jason Lambert has enough sense to make a move before you decide to invite some other man to that cottage who won't act like a gentleman." He let himself kiss her temple and cheek on the way back down to her mouth. "Sweetheart, there aren't just natural threats like wildfire and flash floods to deal with out here. Some of the snakes walk on two legs and are looking for little ladies like you." He let his mouth play over hers in a teasing kiss. "Let's warm up with coffee and have some dessert before I take you home."

Sarah relaxed as they talked in the little ice cream parlor surrounded by families she knew. She felt happy to be seated across from a man who was determined to be her friend. He was suddenly much more than the brash cowboy who flirted furiously and irritated her. Walt was still the most handsome man she'd met in an age, and Sarah wondered what in the world was wrong with her that she didn't just flirt back and go with it. Perhaps all of Julie's escapades with men hadn't taught Julie anything, but her sister took them as cautionary tales and took a giant step back.

Maggie asked Sarah about Walt Stone on Monday morning. "I hear you have a regular date with Walter. He used to shoot birds on your place when no one stayed there." Maggie said it with a little edge to her voice.

Sarah turned around midway through a cut with her dull pastry knife. She used it to gesture as she spoke, "Interesting tidbit of information there, Miss Maggie. The last time you used that tone, I was supposed to be the mother of three, illegitimate children passing myself off as a married woman. Did he happen to use a .38 shotgun when he did that shooting? There's one in my wardrobe upstairs that I just might use on any man who tries to take advantage of me. I am thoroughly done with dating Mr. Stone or anyone else for your information. Walt and I are friends." She smiled in a cutthroat manner.

Maggie frowned, "Did he try to push his luck?"

Sarah laughed, "No, Miss Maggie. Walt is too good for me like most of the men on the planet. In lieu of other young women in this town for girlfriends, I think he and I could be good buddies. He dances a heck of a lot better than any of my old girlfriends anyway and is a good electrician."

Maggie laughed and Sarah growled around the obvious suggestion that she needed a love interest, "Sometimes I wish David Jennings wasn't so damned gay. He's amusing, and we'd make very pretty babies together."

She sobered at Maggie's pale face, "Walt and I agreed to be friends last Friday night; I am actually racking my brain to think of which girlfriend from Boston I'd like to lure here for Thanksgiving who might fall for those great big, brown eyes. That man is ready for marriage and a terribly good catch." She turned around and finished with the dough.

Maggie watched her through the rest of the breakfast service. When Maggie exited in a hurry to talk to Jason Lambert about the menu for a little Halloween party for the family, Sarah grinned and started the luncheon service.

By the end of the day, she received a check for her time saving the firm with the audit and a huge amount for a bonus. There was a note that said, "Thank you for saving us all at Lilac Hill."

When she tried to go into his study to ask him about the bonus because it was thousands of dollars, his father stopped her. Joseph looked down at her, "Sarah, please be patient with us. He is negotiating a new contract and can't be disturbed." Joseph extended a hand to her and walked her down to the dining room and out to the sunroom. He fumbled over a beginning, "I know you may not remember me, but I knew your mother. We spent a great deal of time together as children. She would be so happy to know you and your sister are here with us now."

Sarah resisted the pull of kismet from the grave. "Were you the one who taught me to use the rifle? It's hard to believe I can't remember."

Joseph nodded, "Yes. I might have been your first instructor. Paul Walden lived out there in the little cottage that Jason tells me you are fixing up. Margaret's brother and his second wife took care of the farm a long time." He looked out on the garden but had been transported to another time.

"I have no memory of visiting the mansion when I was little. Why did you visit us at the farm?" she raised her face to look up to Jason's father who must look like Jason should have. Even as an older man, Joseph Lambert was attractive and virile enough to make a woman's heart race. He smiled down into her face.

"I lived there for a time. Isabel threw me out after I admitted to a love affair. I betrayed her and also lost a good friend over that indiscretion. I stayed for two, long summers in the larger house and became quite fond of it. I have never been a saint, Sarah." He carefully examined the woman that he was quite sure his youngest son was mad for in the worst way.

Sarah's eyes flashed, "Did my father know? I don't think he ever came with us when we stayed at Lilac Hill." Their eyes met and Sarah was startled at the deep blue of his eyes watching her with kindness. Sarah felt sudden heat at the insinuation in his eyes. "You are such a cad, Mr. Lambert. Your wife chose to take you back after two years?"

He nodded and kissed her cheek before he left her, "She had our children and was struggling with them alone, so we renewed our vows and became friends like we never were. We married young, Sarah. We weren't cautious like you." He heaved a long sigh and seemed to want to tell her something. Joseph Lambert drooped a bit and added, "Jason would never do such a thing. Be his friend, Sarah, but don't take it too far. He has suffered so much, and I would like to see him happy." He rubbed his beard and squashed ready tears that seemed to afflict him as an old man.

Sarah felt brittle over such confidences, "Happiness is fleeting, Mr. Lambert."

He winced, "You sound like John Monroe."

Sarah nodded. "Yes. My father also said that hurt stays longer and spoils even more. Take care with your loved ones, sir." He took a step back at her intuitive warning. She took the check and deposited it in the bank that day.

By the end of the week, Michael and Walt moved a queen-size plush mattress into her little house. Michael stood outside shuffling uncomfortably while Walt pushed his luck pressing her down on top of it as she stretched on a mattress pad and a fitted sheet. He pinned her so that she could feel how wonderfully matched their bodies were and kissed her neck before fitting his mouth over hers. Sarah kissed him gently and wriggled away as he groaned that he wanted her.

Sliding to stand beside his seated person, Sarah faced him on the bed, "Look Walt. I have three very nice friends coming for Thanksgiving. All of them are available. You'll like one of them more than me."

"I doubt it." He pulled her down onto his lap and kissed her again until they were both prone and melting like chocolate on a warm day. When he lifted off her that time, she lay there panting with large eyes. She made a little sound of protest as he rolled to the side. He cursed and banged out the front door while Michael revved the truck engine.

On the way back to town, Walt grouched to Michael, "I might be able to wear her down some time in the next twenty years." Sarah felt irritated and sticky from the feeling of a man's touch and wanted him to come back all that day and the next. Though it had snowed the night before, Sarah ran Worries Track until it ran with mud.

The next time she saw Walt, she was visiting his parents' house in Lambertville after trick or treating with the children. The Stones invited everyone from the neighborhood in for snacks and a few drinks, so the children could compare candy and do some trading. There was so much silliness among the children and some of the adults who had dressed up to accompany their progeny, the little house hummed with laughter. Sarah was dressed as a gypsy to go with her brood of little wild things.

When she left the children in the kitchen and moved to sit with the adults, she was hardly surprised to see Walt there with a big smile on his face. Sarah relaxed as they talked in the little parlor surrounded by families she knew. She felt happy to be seated across from a man whom she discovered keenly intelligent and determined to be her friend.

That night Walt walked them back to her car parked near the library and casually held her hand. He brushed a kiss at her temple after the kids were seat-belted and whispered, "Tell me a fortune, gypsy woman."

She looked up to him that night but missed his true intention. She grinned at him and whispered back, "You will meet the woman of your dreams on Thanksgiving Day." She stood on tiptoes to kiss him gently.

Walt shook his head, "My parents and I are having Thanksgiving with you at Monroe Farm. I've met you a dozen times.

Some fortune, Sarah. How about, the girl of your dreams will fall into your bed if you just ask real nice?" His mouth played at hers and made her heart beat faster. The kids hooted at them and forced them apart.

Sarah smiled and patted him on the chest. "I'm inviting three of my girlfriends for that weekend, Walt. Each is nicer than the other. You'll meet them on Thanksgiving," she gasped as he hauled her close to his body and leaned over her for a kiss that melted her to unthinking blinks at him. It was so intense, the children just watched with mesmerized shock on their faces.

He was rough-voiced, and she felt his rocky anger, "I don't want anyone but you. Get that through your thick head, Sarah Monroe." He let her go abruptly and turned away from her to walk back up the street toward his parents' home. His head was down, and he looked like he was muttering.

CHAPTER 14

Conundrum

Thanksgiving brought Sarah's friends from Boston to Lambertville on a four-day visit that turned the farm on its ear. Julie was given a glimpse of Sarah's more open personality than the quiet, serious one Sarah had adopted since the move to the farm. The trio of Nancy, Michaela and Georgiana arrived with laughter and giddy relief after the road trip. Nancy, the exhausted driver with a whip-like tongue and severely cut, short, black hair, declared that the farm was truly perched at the edge of the world, and pulled out maps because she was not driving anywhere near the Washington Beltway again. Michaela Ritchie recounted trips their usual trio had taken to New York, weekends at a borrowed cottage on the Vineyard and crazy bar crawls through Boston. Georgiana Ensky of the Boston Ensky clan quickly took to flirting with Walt Stone at Sarah's bidding. Georgiana's older brother drove up from North Carolina where he was finishing his degree.

"Georgie" was pinup pretty with long legs, bright russet-hued hair that naturally curled down her back and an eager grin that said she rarely suffered for anything. She toured the town on her brother's arm and admired its quaint architecture, the beautiful park that meandered with the river that ran through the valley and the shabby, grandeur of Lilac Hill. Sarah watched her friend for any signs of condescension like she'd noticed in the two other girls she invited for the long weekend, but Georgie was charmed by the place. If her brother Tom hadn't cornered Sarah in the small, back bedroom she fixed up for his use during the visit, the entire holiday would have been enjoyable. Tom went back to college with a shiner, and Walt sped back to town on Thanksgiving angry with the entire Monroe contingent.

Joseph Lambert could not sleep. He rose by 2 a.m.

convinced that he would never sleep a whole night again. He relived the scenes of his life, and regret wracked every part of it. Cases he had forgotten were tried again. He rethought charges to clients, his speeches before every judge and the odd situations when he knew he'd slipped. Slipping was the label he had for sloppiness of any type.

Sloppiness had resulted in the birth of Sarah Monroe. He watched his son Jason fall in love with her but ignored it all that summer. When she gave all of them the cold shoulder after her brother-in-law returned, Joseph was relieved. Joseph prayed that she'd fall in love with that tall truck driver she dated a few times, but Sarah seemed oddly resistant to the charms of any man. When she brought a bevy of young men and women into town on the day after Thanksgiving, he hoped that one of them was her distraction. He prayed she'd go home to Boston, and yet in his heart, he was gratified that she stayed. Sarah Monroe was the image of her mother and his own dark looks combined.

Joseph Lambert walked the garden in the dark cold of early December and felt unsure. Sarah's mother had been a shorter woman and fair like her eldest daughter, but her grandfather had been willow thin with a slippery grace like Sarah. He wondered over Sarah's tendency toward fidgety athleticism and thought of his own youth running these hills. He watched her hair spring wavy and deeply auburn brown just like his before it faded to gray. Those deep, blue eyes had looked at him so critically and cautioned him about love. Couldn't she see the shade of her own eyes reflected back in his? Joseph Lambert had taken a huge gamble when he accepted the offer from John Monroe for the farm at Lilac Hill. He had imagined Elizabeth coming home to the little farm she had visited each summer to see her reclusive father. Had John Monroe tried to buy the place out of some weird revenge that was diabolically resolving itself?

Joseph Lambert walked the gardens until he heard her car pull up the drive and into her accustomed place in the staff lot. He turned and looked to the kitchen where the lights were being turned on one by one as she opened it up and lent it her careful warmth. His fingers twitched over telling Sarah Monroe the truth before she opened her arms to his blissfully ignorant son Jason. Ed Wakelin had kidded with Isabel and Joseph about Jason's flirtation with their little pastry chef just before he'd been arrested. At the time, Joseph had squashed the alarm that reports of their passionate embrace had created in his gut. Joseph Lambert brushed away the constant bile of panic in his throat and padded through the gardens to go in and speak the truth to his daughter Sarah.

"Sarah, I told you I was indiscreet and lived at your farm on Lilac Hill for a few summers?" He was fiddling with the belt to his robe while Sarah watched his every move. After being pressed toward intimacy by both Walt Stone and Georgiana's brother over the weekend, Sarah was more than cautious about men. At the moment, she found lust a bothersome distraction to real friendship. Jason Lambert would barely look at her, yet he had asked her to work on their accounts again because he hadn't hired a real bookkeeper. When they met privately, she understood from his body language that all she had to do was invite him, and he would come across with embraces like she replayed in her head from October.

Sarah nodded at Joseph Lambert and poured him a coffee. She tried to hand it to him, but he couldn't take it because his hands were shaking. "Sir, are you feeling sick? You're trembling."

Jason had been hovering in the hallway unsure of his father's motives for speaking to Sarah alone. He came into the kitchen and placed a hand on his father's wrist. "Dad, what's wrong?"

Joseph felt the weight of not going back or giving excuses to prolong his agony over warning them. "Sarah, the woman with whom I betrayed Isabel was your mother." He sounded ridiculously formal, so Sarah giggled and shook her head to dismiss it. He spoke up more sure, "It wasn't a true affair; it was one evening among all the years I wanted her. We were together twenty-six years ago on an August night. You could be my daughter." His eyes watered and fell to his slippers as both of them gasped.

"I went to your father the next morning and asked him to let her go. I told your father that I would stand by her if she became pregnant, but he beat me senseless and took your mother home to Trenton. I begged her to return to me at Lilac Hill. I visited, called and wrote her letters. She finally wrote me and told me to go back to Isabel. She wrote that she loved John Monroe." He looked back up with eyes shining, "But she brought you back here when you turned two. I knew the moment I saw you; I'd reconciled with Isabel, and I just could not break her heart again."

Sarah shook her head, "No. You're wrong. John Monroe was my father. He was the kindest man I've ever known. He showed us he loved us every day. He loved my mother, and it broke his heart when she died." Sarah reached up and took Joseph Lambert by either shoulder in a fierce grip and shook him once. "I warned you to be careful with your loved ones, sir. Hurt spreads like cancer." She let him go and stepped back to glare at father and son.

Her eyes pleaded with Jason to step up and say something. She met blue eyes that had looked familiar to her from their first meeting. She looked at his thin lips like hers and the deep brown of his hair so much like hers. How could he suddenly look so much like a brother? She shook her head to wipe out the beginnings of clearer sight. She turned away from both of them and began her day's baking.

Maggie Turner was back to watching Sarah Monroe carefully. She had seen Sarah's sister on their first weekend three years ago shopping at the grocery store. She had stopped dead and stared at the young version of Elizabeth Walden Monroe, her brother's oldest daughter. It was uncanny that the skinny child with a mop of straggly hair and big teeth would grow into a soft, white-skinned, blue-eyed woman with voluptuous curves. Maggie had followed the new Elizabeth around the store like she wore a homing device for estranged family. It was obvious that the Julie had no idea what her shape was doing to the male customers or what her identity was doing to Maggie.

Then Sarah Monroe had been delivered to the kitchen as her sister's opposing pole. Sarah had dark looks, not only thick, deep brown tresses but the silence of the inner turn she remembered in her older brother. Paul Walden had been a stern, unyielding man who ruled his family like a tyrant. Maggie had left her father's house for marriage at sixteen and had seen little of Paul until he took the caretaker's job at Lilac Hill after a mining accident left him one leg and a pension.

Paul's little girls had turned into pretty, young things by then and attracted boys from Wheeling and all the way from Charleston. Elizabeth Walden and Joseph Lambert had been seen walking the woods a number of times the spring he became engaged to Isabel Trehearne, a rich, educated Northerner whose father offered Joseph a partnership. Nobody was surprised when Elizabeth jilted her lover Joseph Lambert for a tall, blond college man from Wheeling after she heard rumors about the impending engagement. When John Monroe moved his wife to New Jersey, nobody blinked an eye. Everyone was moving to the city for jobs during the 1960s.

Elizabeth and her family wrote to Paul often and visited every summer. Maggie thought of picnics and family suppers when they returned to Wheeling or Lambertville for little reunions. Maggie's brother Paul had been injured the winter that John Monroe first asked to buy the farm at Lilac Hill to use as a home for his father-in-law and a retreat for his family. They had a little girl who was blond just like he and Elizabeth.

Joseph Lambert must have been tantalized by the prospect of seeing his Elizabeth each time the family visited. He had two fine boys of his own with Isabel Trehearne. Whenever the Monroe family visited, sparks flew and finally Isabel forced Joseph Lambert to choose between his family and his first love. For two years, Joseph Lambert stayed at the farm on Lilac Hill in a pout. When he returned, he never strayed again.

Isabel had insisted on a permanent move to New York which left the mansion empty for fifteen years except for the caretakers and infrequent vacations.

Maggie watched prickly Sarah Monroe baking in the small kingdom of the Lambert kitchen. She had never spoken to Sarah about being her aunt. The Walden family was rife with eccentrics like her brother Paul who might not have been introduced to the little girls as their grandfather. When Elizabeth had teased and seduced Joseph Lambert the year she turned 32, Maggie had been Isabel's sounding board. The rift between the families was never healed after the affair. Maggie had commiserated with Isabel and turned a deaf ear on her own brother's wife when she tried to make sense of the turmoil in Elizabeth's family. In the end, Paul had thrown up his hands and huffed, "Women!" but he was kind to the little girls when their mother visited every summer.

Maggie remembered her father saying that a healed over wound should never be lanced for cleaning. Watching Sarah's steady withdraw from animation again after the thaw from the fire on Lilac Hill, Maggie's heart ached. This was not a problem to take to Isabel in her precarious health. She was angry with Joseph Lambert and his urge to confess every hurtful thing during these last years of his life. Jason was more immersed in his work now that he was afraid to love Sarah Monroe.

Sarah finally took her problem to Julie who just stared at her for a few minutes to digest it. They took out the boxes of family photo albums and rummaged until they found pictures of their mother looking as beautiful and full of life as Julie. They found a few of their grandparents, so Sarah could examine the stern looks of the Monroe ancestors and then grimace into a mirror for similarities. Neither could believe that the hermit they remembered serving as the grouchy caretaker at the farm was actually Paul Walden, their grandfather. They looked at birth certificates and shrugged at each other. For once, Sarah let a crying jag envelop her. Julie hugged her sister and rubbed her back until Sarah fell asleep with her head on Julie's lap like a little child. When Michael came in from picking the kids up from school, they sent everyone to their rooms, so the three adults could discuss the question.

Michael suggested DNA testing to ease everyone's mind. He looked at the two women as a composition of light and dark, soft and hard. He teased Sarah, "It's not a problem if you forget flirting with Lambert and decide to fall for Walt Stone. I know you meant well inviting all those little flirty skirts up here for Thanksgiving, Sarah, but I think he's pretty damned mad at you for trying to palm him off like leftovers. He is that angry kind of hurt. He has it bad for you." Michael's face softened when he talked about Walt; he actually thought it impossible that Walt preferred dour-faced Sarah to the pretty women she paraded all over town during Thanksgiving week. They had been lovely girls with diverse interests and talents any man might find interesting. The redhead had been so taken with the town and the scenery that she looked into jobs before she left for Boston.

Sarah frowned at him but understood his concern, "I just don't want to repeat the past, Michael. I don't think I'm ready for love yet—no matter who it is." She felt bad for hurting Walt Stone. The poor man had been nothing but kind and warm to her cold, hard self. He had been there for her sister and the children. It made her throat thick with regret. She saw him at the town events and during weekly library visits. She made up her mind to be kinder to him when next they met.

Sarah asked Joseph Lambert to arrange for a DNA test and told him again that John Monroe was her father. She dreamed of her father again, and he had the same sad look that Walt had worn the last time they met for coffee, and she apologized for being a poor friend. She wrote down snatches of the advice her father told her in dreams. When she ran, the words became mantras. *Run your own race. Trust yourself. Look out for your sister. Remember that I love you.*

The next weekend she took Walt with her to a big dance hall event with her cousins in Wheeling just to warm up his regard for her a bit. She tried not to think of the date as a weird insurance. This time when Walt pulled her closer, she let herself enjoy his warmth and rested her head on his shoulder. His kisses were gentle but coursed electric through her spine and began to melt deep inhibitions that had walled up her heart.

Sarah Monroe ran every day that December on Worries Track despite slashing rain, intermittent sleet, bone-chilling air or odd evenings of dense fog. Annabelle sometimes ran a lap or two with her just to see how it felt to run away from your problems. Robby tried it and told his sisters, "You don't run away from the worries. Sarah says the running untangles them." Julie smiled when she heard that and imagined fields full of unknotted yarn from all the challenges Sarah had faced in one brief year.

Sarah's mind was brimming with recipes, struggles over some of Jason's accounting, fighting with Julie finally, arguing with Michael, her own personal accounting, dancing with Walt Stone, Robby's difficulty with reading, kissing Jason just one night, Leanne learning to pronounce her consonants, kissing Walt again after asking to work on their friendship and missing being scolded by Jason. She could sometimes see a clear path through some trouble only after her muscles burned and her lungs ached.

Leanne confided to Walt Stone after dinner with the family one night. "I'm worried that Sarah might start running straight and wind up right back in Boston. That pretty far north, isn't it?"

Walter stroked the curls springing out of Leanne's ponytail and told her that he didn't think Sarah would ever go back to Boston. Her aunt was putting down roots. He watched Sarah washing dishes next to Michael and laughing with him over some silliness. They had battled with each other while under the same roof, but just a quarter mile apart, they were becoming friends.

Walt Stone thought about Sarah and decided he had been going about attracting her all wrong. That night he abruptly kissed both women good night and waved to Michael. They didn't see or hear from Walt Stone for two weeks. When Sarah bumped into him at the library with the children, he seemed eager to get away. Sarah bit her lip and regretted losing his attention and then chided herself because she had encouraged him to stay away.

When she ran, her returning worry unconsciously became Walt Stone. So when they danced next at a little gathering in town for Billy's birthday, Sarah looked up to him and paid close attention to a little story about his distributorship in Wheeling. He raised an eyebrow at her attention and brushed a kiss on her cheek at the end of the dance, "What's wrong, Sarah?"

Sarah Monroe wanted to act casual and shield her thoughts, but she blurted out, "I have been worried about you, Walt." He looked down at her and cocked one eyebrow again.

Walt had half-bowed to her and said, "Good." He raised her hand to his mouth and then led her back to her family. When she turned around to ask for another dance, he was out on the dance floor with a pretty blonde who worked with Julie at the mine.

Michael smirked but asked Sarah to dance. Walt ignored her even after Billy handed her off to Jason Lambert. Sarah's mouth angled down as she and Jason bickered over this and that as they danced. When they disappeared together, Walt followed and watched Lambert walk her to her car and give her a chaste hug before she slipped behind the wheel and drove away.

Stepping out of the shadows, Walt approached Lambert with an extended hand which Jason shook without reservation. "So Sarah is holding you off, too?" Walt was a bit surprised because he had sensed a simmering heat between them from the beginning.

Jason laughed, "Think of us as siblings, Walt. I feel protective of her like you do." Lambert thrust his hands in his pockets and rocked back on his heels. "I know you're a good guy, Walt. What was up tonight? Are you playing hard to get after drooling all over her last summer?"

Walt smiled sheepishly but shook his head, "Patience is a

virtue, I've heard. I thought I should back off for a while." He thrust his hands in his pockets like Jason and kicked at the gravel. "Mr. Lambert? Sarah invited three girlfriends up here from Boston and paraded them in front of me for Thanksgiving. I actually joked with Michael in front of her about having the red-head for dessert."

Jason laughed out loud, "What was Sarah's reaction?"

Walt was smiling in earnest now because talking to Jason put it all in perspective, "She slipped on her track shoes and ran for an hour. That red-headed girl, Judy or Georgie, did you meet her? She told me Sarah just fell into bed that night without changing and slept until she had to go to work."

Jason smirked, "Incredible girl if you can catch her, Walt. Think for a moment about her reaction to you. I'd bet that she will be out there at dawn racing around the track after tonight. The hell with patience. Get out there and bring her breakfast; do something for her that she might not expect." Jason looked at Walt eye-to-eye, "You are a good man, Walt Stone."

Walter nodded, "Thank you, sir. That means something coming from you."

CHAPTER 15

Stone's Patio

Walter Stone raided the grocery store that evening for everything he might need and loaded the grill from his garage into the back of the truck. At four o'clock in the morning, he pulled past the main house of Monroe Farm and drove directly around her cottage to the back door. December was spongy wet, and the skies threatened snow over the next ridge. He waved at her figure on the track in the rear field that he remembered planted with spring strawberries, summer peas and autumn cabbage for many years. Sarah was sowing troubles and pain in that circle she traversed. She barely slowed when she recognized the truck, and he took her continued running as frustration with his attitude.

They had talked months ago about a stone patio for the back of the house where she might build a lattice to create an outdoor dining area surrounded by flowering vines. She and Michael had hovered over pictures her friends brought with them from a trip to northern Italy. Walt lifted the shovel out of the back of the truck and began to level the area Sarah and Michael had marked with large uneven stones they collected from the area.

Sarah finished her run, ambled back to watch Walt and cast a glance at the contents of the truck. She started to touch the stack of fieldstone near the tailgate. His voice, winded from the exertion, stopped her, "Leave that. Get yourself some breakfast and make some coffee, could you?"

"Can I help or will I be in the way?" She looked at him with a mulish expression. This was not how she'd planned to spend her day.

Walt shrugged, "It's your patio. There's an extra shovel in the truck, and I know you have gloves. Get your regulation yogurt and then slip on some boots. Don't want to ruin your sneakers," he smiled slightly when he said that.

Sarah smiled broadly and saluted him, "Yes, sir, Mr. Stone." When she returned in ten minutes, she had changed into beaten jeans and old boots. He grinned behind her back as she began clearing and leveling the area that was the size of a small room. As they spread the layer of soil she and Michael had hauled from a construction site advertising free fill dirt, Walt started to talk her through the reasons for the layer of raked smooth dirt.

He knew her shoulders must be aching, and her back was burning like his, but he kept his voice calm and quiet. He did not caution her not to overdo it, and did not tease her when she left him to retrieve drinks for both of them.

Michael appeared at ten, half-dressed and grumbling over ridiculous Sunday morning activities. They discussed the rocks and stones they'd gathered, placed them carefully and then unloaded a whole series of flagstone Walt had picked up at Lamberts' that morning. Sarah did not ask questions but looked slightly teary-eyed.

When Julie peeked around the house, she urged Sarah to run into the house and get a shower; they were expected at church by noon. Julie looked at the two men and frowned, "You two are absolved from required attendance today on account of good works." As soon as Sarah was safely inside the house, Julie gave Walt a tap on the back and cautioned, "You are taking your chances. What's the plan?" Her eyes were wicked and delighted with him.

Walt pushed back his hat and wiped the sweat off his face. He was thankful that it was only 45 degrees that day. "Just a little cookout for two, Julie. Harmless."

Julie nodded and glanced at her husband, "Michael, I believe your mother and father would like to see the kids today. Could you call them while I'm at church?"

Michael grunted in agreement. He paused as the car hesitated for a moment before turning left onto the old county road. "Those Monroe girls are something, Walt. Julie is the most beautiful woman on the planet even in her plain dress for Sunday services." He looked back to the woods climbing

Lilac Hill and smiled. "I'm a lucky man."

After the children left to visit their grandparents, Sarah returned to the back of the cottage and put on her work clothes
again. Sarah helped Walt spread the sand over the rocks and
flagstone after a flurry of placing, removing, digging and filling
and then repositioning each great weight. He explained, "We
might have to move some of them after the winter, but we'll
let the whole thing settle till spring." Sarah bit her lip over the
thought of another spring at Lilac Hill.

Both Walt and Sarah were winded and achy by the time
they finished the patio and sat on the back steps with a glass
of water each. Walt nudged her with his shoulder when she
snuck a glance at him with a question on her face, "What?"

"No fighting. Walt, we did this without one argument." He
agreed with a grunt of pleasure. Of course they hadn't fought;
he rarely needed to push differences with anyone, least of all
Sarah. He looked at the stone patio and squinted to find defi-
ciencies.

The snow clouds that had been on the western horizon
were encroaching into their valley. Walt stood and stretched
before crossing to a form shrouded in a tarp that he and Michael had removed from the truck while she was at church. He
pulled it onto the flattest area and untied the tarp. It revealed
a shiny, gas grill that he'd bought on a whim last fall. There was
a slim likelihood that he'd ever use it at his house with his time
on the road and preoccupation with his parents. He fiddled
with it and managed to light it just like the instructions said
it would.

He turned to Sarah and explained, "I thought I'd cook for
you. A bit of switching roles because you always cook." He
turned off the grill and sighed, "But first I need a shower. Do
you want me to use the one in the main house?"

Sarah let her hands rise to her hips, "You may use my
shower, Walt Stone. But I need to find you soap that doesn't
smell like flowers first." She gave him a teasing smile as they
walked into the house together. He'd removed a gym bag from

the truck.

He jiggled the bag, "I came prepared. No worry, I'll be quick." Sarah stood in the hallway and stared at the closed door thinking about Walter coming out to the house with this gift of a day. He had given her a day of toil and companionship. As much as he made her mouth water after all this patient time, she was loath to ruin it by slipping under the shower with him though she did it in a little daydream. She made a cake while he showered, but she was on fire before she even turned the oven to bake.

While she showered, he lit the grill and lifted the cooler he'd packed that morning from the truck. He rolled his sore shoulders and bounced a little side to side to loosen the muscles in his thighs. Driving the truck this week would be uncomfortable, but it was worth it just to have the little conversation they'd just traded on the porch steps. He glanced up into the afternoon sky which was graying fast and rolled his head to ease tightening neck muscles.

After the grill warmed up, he placed the potatoes just like his mother made them straight from a brine soak into aluminum wrap and checked the marinated steaks. When Sarah came out of the house and approached with two glasses of red wine, he cocked an eyebrow and approved of her choice, "We're having steak."

He toasted her silently and appreciated that she'd changed into a skirt and soft sweater. Her damp hair unbound was full, a lush streaky auburn to walnut silk. He watched her pull a small table off the porch, so he had a staging area for cooking.

She looked up at the sky and saw the snow clouds threatening. "You brought a patio, a grill and dinner?" Sarah had been convinced the night before that she'd chased him away for good. "Why?"

Walt heaved out a breath that he held to contain his impatience with her, "If I have to explain, this has been a total waste. Go back into the house and bring a few plates out in twenty minutes. Take a nap or something, but please leave me alone for a bit, Sarah." Walt had let his irritation loose with his words. Obediently, Sarah retreated to the house, set the table and lay on the divan with the intention of resting her eyes.

When Walt stomped into the house to retrieve plates a half hour later, he stopped at the bottom of the old couch and kicked at it once, "Hey, wake up and come out to help bring this in. It's starting to snow, sweetheart." His voice had roughened over her relaxed form in a sleeping sprawl. It flitted through his mind that she was all arms and legs and would probably dominate a bed.

She startled out of the nap and followed him out to a quick twilight as snow clouds clogged the valley. The meal was fragrant, and her stomach grumbled just like his. Walt knew he'd be bone-tired later, but at the moment, he was filled with the excitement of a plan brought to fruition. He placed a number of filled plates before him and gave Sarah an empty one. He sipped at his wine that she had refilled. She sat at her empty plate and eyed him warily. "What's the game, Walt?"

He shrugged, "I watched you feed little tastes of the Thanksgiving meal to Julie, Michael, your guests, and the kids. A forkful here, a bit of a spoon there until they sat at the table so ravenous that it was passion not hunger for filling the belly that drove them to eat what they really wanted."

Walt uncovered a plate with long slices of grilled zucchini with roasted tomatoes. He sliced a bite for her and offered it. She leaned forward and took it from the fork. He did the same and watched her face. She rolled it around in her mouth and emitted a little grunt of pleasure, "Yes. It's delicate."

He smiled and gave her a slice on her plate, "Portabella without the price tag. Next, baked potato soaked for a day in brine with no butter." This she leaned forward and took from his fingers into her mouth.

His breath caught at the slight linger of her mouth on his fingers, and he warned her, "No teasing. I am ravenous for you, Sarah." She sat back but arched a brow at his warning. She stilled herself to patience through all his teasing with the dishes he'd prepared for her. While they ate side-by-side, Sarah had the urge to cry, and so she did.

Walt slid an arm around her back but kept eating in silence. The little downpour was brief, and he dropped his hold to pour her more wine. "A bit tired, Sarah?"

She shook her head and finished her meal. She snuck regular glances at him as they cleaned up the meal and divided the leftovers into a lunch for him and a dinner for her. She made coffee and invited him to sit down on the couch while it perked.

When she caught him rolling his shoulders as she washed the wine glasses, she dried her hands and stood before him. She gestured for him to sit forward and stood between his knees to rub the knots out of his neck and shoulders. He shuddered from the pleasure of her hands on his body like he'd imagined for months. He was cresting over the waves of pain when she squeezed the muscles and released them. She dared to kiss his forehead, his temple, cheek and chin.

Sarah whispered, "Thank you. No one has ever cooked for me, Walt. This day was a most precious gift."

He looked up at her as she ran her hands down his arms; he wanted to hold onto her waist and pull her toward him. He waited as she gave him a soft look and lowered her mouth to his for a lazy, enveloping kiss. Then he stood up and stretched, kissed her again lightly and moved toward his boots at the door, "I'll cover up the grill and bring the table back up. I'd better get down the road before the snow gets too deep."

Sarah blinked at him, but she followed him back out to their stone patio, and helped to bring in the table and extra plates and tools. She stood at his truck with snow landing in her hair. He hesitated only a moment before starting it. She looked at the ghost of a road leading away from the cottage, "Call me when you get home, Walt. I worry about you on the road."

Walt shook his head, "I'll call, but don't worry over me, Sarah. Just go out with me the next time I ask. Good night, sweetheart." He was gone down the lane carefully staying on the gravel path all the way to the main road. When he called later and proposed pizza after the library with the kids that week,

Sarah laughed and said yes. She had never known a man who improved with familiarity before Walt Stone.

CHAPTER 16

Visiting Home

The arrival of real snow in the valley did not fill Sarah with the joy it had in Boston. In the city, the white layer pretended to cleanse the streets, buildings and parks. It erased the shadows of the tall buildings and swept the neighborhoods, so for a few brief hours, everything was new. In the city, her goal would have been getting outside, so she could stamp the freshness into her senses before the inevitable, dirty clean up sometimes only hours later. In Lambertville, the newness was there, so she enjoyed the first flush of excitement over it, but snow soon became a worry because of the ice layer beneath and the fragile grip of the tires on the road. She scrambled to find boots for the children and wondered which box contained her heavier coat. The weight of responsibility returned after the high of Michael's return and the vanquishing of the CPA exam. It filtered down in snowflakes and cemented in hail and ice storms.

Sarah's removal to Lavender Cottage which was nothing but a work in progress. She rose the day after building her lovely patio with Walt Stone and stared at the ghost of his grill on the obliterated plain where they'd worked in grim sympathy. She sipped her coffee and rolled her shoulders at four in the morning. She flicked on the flood lights just to stare at the outline of their work and to think about his muscles under her fingers. She smiled at his careful offering of a meal made on top of a day of labor. She frowned at wanting him there to run a hand over her back and soothe her tight muscles. A steady thrumming like the vibration of her feet on the hollow earth started at the center of her belly. It vibrated through her and made her want to hum.

Why had she been so cold with that man? Despite his obvious, rough good looks and completely tongue-tied affection for her, despite his foolishness with his buddies in the bar, he proved consistent, warm and considerate in the most baffling way—a deep, endless way that accepted all of her hard edges, her distance and her fragile tension. If she stopped battling her attraction to him, Walt Stone would melt in her arms out of sheer relief.

She stared out at the patio under a good three feet of snow and rolled her shoulders again and stopped suddenly. Had he installed the floodlights one week night while she was at the library with the kids or was it one of the first evenings she was away meeting with clients? He'd told her never to step out the door until she startled the wild things that lived in that untamed section before the firebreak and woods. She remembered stumbling in October over the snake on her run and wondered if he was shining a light on her before stepping into her domain. Sarah growled at Walt Stone's manipulation of her wild independence, turned off the flood lights and dressed to shovel. She attach chains Michael had found for her tires last week and maneuvered the little car up the road. She silently cursed Walt Stone for every achy muscle that reminded her of the pleasure of his company. She hoped he was feeling tortured just like her.

After Sarah had started the coffee and the ovens, Jason Lambert appeared the kitchen, phoned Maggie and told her to stay home that day. "I don't want you out on the road for the first snowfall. Sarah's here." Sarah turned back to readying bread dough.

Jason sipped at his coffee and watched her knead and pat. She placed the dough into a bowl and covered it. She began the pastry dough but stilled when she heard him cross the small space between stations. Sarah wasn't even surprised when he slipped his arms around her waist and pulled her against his chest. He whispered like he had months ago, "Sarah, turn around and talk to me." She let herself rest there and enjoy the way his warmth invaded her back and met the thrumming core that Walt Stone had put there.

Jason opened his hands on her belly and rested his face on her neck between her head and her shoulder. His lips brushed her ear, and Sarah carefully released the dough she was squeezing the resiliency out of and turned to face him. He kissed her with such longing that she felt devoured. She stiffened over their weird fit; she had not felt uncomfortable with Walt. Jason's fingers ran over her back and pressed her so close that she wondered if she had fallen into some chasm in him that needed filling.

"Sarah," he whispered. "Sarah, I want you, but I can't have you." He looked at her closely and found the blue eyes of his sister. He ran a finger over the tight angle of her cheek and pulled her hand up to run her fingers over his unmarked left cheek. He began to smile in his lop-sided way, "You have unlocked something inside me, Sarah. All that damned-up, quiet strength in you met me and shook me until I was free. Thank you, little sister."

He hauled her into his arms as her eyes reflected the hurt, and she dissolved into sheer sorrow over his revelation. She cried quietly, locked in his arms as he smoothed over her tense shoulders, back, and arms with warm hands. She knew she was melting like the snow in an avalanche of pained confusion. Her father's advice repeated itself to her in his voice and steadied her, "I know she's older, but look out for your sister," and "Sarah, you are so smart and strong; run your own race." Sarah sighed and stopped crying. She rested her head on Jason Lambert's chest understanding the deep attraction to him should have caused her alarm, and it had.

When Joseph and Isabel Lambert wandered into the kitchen looking for breakfast, they watched her straighten up and pin her shoulders back. She rested her head on Jason's shoulder as he told his parents the results of the DNA test. Isabel nodded and extended a hand to Sarah, "If I ever wanted a daughter, I hoped she would be strong like you."

Sarah nodded to them, but she could not begin to accept it, "Thank you, Miss Isabel. What would you like for breakfast? I believe I'm taking requests this morning." Sarah forced her rough voice to stab at humor because she had been afraid of this revelation for a month. She could not even raise her eyes to look at Joseph Lambert with John Monroe's voice speaking to her still. She nearly fled to walk the gardens, but that would have meant a trudge through the snow, and she was incredibly tired.

Isabel and Sarah made the family breakfast, and for the first time, she sat in the dining room with them and ate some fruit with her morning yogurt. She looked at Jason Lambert and saw the handsome, attractive man he was under the veil of scars. She prayed a little thank you to the spirit, the inclination really, not to seduce him completely in Ed Wakelin's office when it would have been so easy. She chided herself to trust her instincts, so she rose, collected plates and returned to the kitchen to begin the lunch that Maggie had ordered before snow dropped its blanket on the area.

CHAPTER 17

The Journey Back

Christmas should have been easier with waking up to loving Walt even if the emotion was tempered with a grudge. Sarah was a bit angry at falling so hard for his manipulation of her desires for independence and hard work. When he showed up with a tractor to scrape away the new foot and a half of snow from the Monroe drive two days later, he tossed her the keys and asked, "Want instructions before I get up the road, or do you want to figure it out yourself?" He'd gone from vaguely hurt to brashly confident in only one day.

Sarah put her hands on her hips and muttered, "Don't tease me."

As they were walking to the trailer to back the tractor onto a path she'd cleared for Julie's old Jeep, he reached out a hand for her. He brought her up short and hauled her into his arms for a breathless, cold kiss. "That's for torturing me all day Monday. Every time my muscles ached, I wanted your hands on me like Sunday night." He stopped himself from saying something about love because she was warmer yet grouchy for some reason. He smiled down at her, but he was working the puzzle of her sharp edges.

Sarah kissed him back with a bit of the anger expelled, "Monday morning, I decided you made me hurt so badly on purpose. Every ache is you torturing me." She slid off her gloves to touch his face with her finger tips; "Staying for dinner, Walt?" She was examining the anguish in his face when she dared to touch him.

He squeezed her so tight it made her gasp, "Not today, sweetheart." Another achy kiss. "My parents need some tending. There was more snow in the valley than here on the mountain. You stay put and work your place. We'll have another day." He sighed at that and looked up into skies that were thick and gray with further snow threats. Sarah gazed up at him and recognized the caretaker's soul in the man that was just as strong as hers. He put all of them before himself like she did each time a challenge arrived. She rested her cheek on his coat and hugged him back.

So with the promise of Walt and the warm acceptance of the Lamberts, Christmas should have been joyful. On Christmas Eve, Walt was on the road for the busiest day of the season. Julie and Mike were fighting like most couples do struggling to make the holiday a dream come true, and the children were strung out and scrapping like cats. Sarah walked the melted, brooding gardens at the Lambert Mansion during her one o'clock break. In one terrible argument with Joseph Lambert, Sarah had refused to be introduced as his daughter. She thought of Christmas morning and felt the low, sharp pain in her belly that had been absent for months.

She used the phone in the kitchen to leave a message for Walt. "I won't be home for Christmas. I'm visiting home for a few days," she garbled in to the recording because she was mentally driving out of the valley and trying not to cry. The note she left for Julie with her gifts for the children read, "Julie, I am visiting our parents. Be back for work on Monday. Merry Christmas, big sister. I love you. Sarah" The signature was a blur because her tears had dropped on the note there.

Christmas was a storm of irritation for Walt because he visited Monroe Farm with his parents to deliver gifts for the children and left his gift for Sarah on her kitchen table. He'd given her new track shoes with a note that said in careful script, "Run to me. I love you. Walt Stone." He nearly crumpled up the note but patted the ring box in his jacket pocket. The ring had nothing to do with the holiday; it had to do with keeping her on Worries Track and not barreling through the valley away from him like she was doing at that moment. He found himself angry all over again at Sarah's rough urge for independence because it sliced her away from him. He and Michael threw back a few beers and groused to each other about women to keep themselves from going after Sarah Monroe.

Sarah took her time getting to Trenton. She stopped at a diner in Maryland and read the little pamphlets there while she ate eggs and toast because they rolled their eyes at her request for yogurt. There was a lake resort nearby and skiing. She smiled grimly and thought about the skiing her little car had done on the drive to the Lambert Mansion every day that week. Living through the winter with the little car was going to be a trial. She ordered a chicken sandwich wrapped to go from that place and refilled a thermos with hot coffee. She was worried that everything would be closed by the time she reached Trenton. She could crash at any of her friends' homes once she arrived in the old neighborhood, but the desire for solitude was strong.

Her thoughts were so busy that she failed to listen to the radio most of the way up the coast bearing east. When she finally switched it on for the weather, she pressed the buttons and realized that she couldn't remember any of the old stations she'd listened to her whole life until Boston and then Lambertville. She remembered nothing but West Virginia or Pennsylvania call letters and the little Cumberland station that came through stronger in the morning. She knew her life had been honed into the strong bonds and clean lines of the children, Julie and Michael, the Lamberts and Walt in a bare six months. Thinking of them made her warm all the way through and insulated her from the icy sleet that was obliterating her view through the windshield between wiper swipes.

Once she reached Trenton, Sarah still took her time. She drove past her parents' old house to circle around the block to the church and noted times for worship which hadn't changed. She parked and walked up the hill to the grade school. She stared for a bit at the playground and the hill they'd used for sledding. She returned to the church and sat in one of the back pews for part of a Mass thinking about all the years she'd studied the stained glass, made all the right responses but hadn't actually felt prayer until the forest burned on Lilac Hill. Sarah studied the families gathered for the one o'clock service with fidgety children, old people with canes supporting their bent backs, and parents creased with exhaustion. It was hard work being a family; Sarah's heart was weighted with the effort and the joy of that toil.

Then she drove out of town to the cemetery and walked its perimeter to work her way in by memory to her parents' double stone. She placed a bouquet of dried herbs and wildflowers from her first garden at Lilac Hill on her father's side. At her mother's, she positioned a jar of the jam she and Julie had made with all three children before Michael returned.

She sat on the ground after squatting for a few minutes and removing debris from nearly a year's absence. She brushed a gloved hand over John Monroe's name and then her mother's side of the stone with a thickened throat. Slowly Sarah began to recite the story of her move to Lilac Hill. She told her father about everything that had happened since she left Boston in May. She thanked him for the encouragement he had always offered. She recited the dishes that she'd made thinking he might have enjoyed them. She mulled over regrets but found fewer than she'd counted all the way up the road from Lambertville.

Sarah shifted to her mother's name and squinted. She asked her mother, "How could you have ever loved Joseph Lambert? Couldn't you see the shallow, vain thing he was? What kind of man was he under all that money and pretense?" Her voice dried up. The man lying beside her mother was so fine just like Walt. "John Monroe and Walt Stone are men who only come once in a lifetime," she cautioned flighty Elizabeth Walden Monroe. In a flash, Sarah felt love flood all the way through her body into her tight soul. She finished her thoughts in a rough voice, "Oh Mama, I hope we haven't broken their hearts with all this selfishness."

With the sleet peppering her hood and icy snow melting under her cold bottom, Sarah sat teary but satisfied at the gravestones. When she looked up, she saw other singletons, couples and families arriving, pausing and leaving their loved ones. There was no panic or intense heartache like the other visits since her mother died six years ago. She could drive the five hours back to West Virginia without feeling out of control like she had on the quick visit here on the way from Boston last May.

Sarah stood up and brushed off what she could of the frozen slush on her clothes and gathered the dried grass, old flowers and leaves. She walked over the ridge and visited the graves of friends and neighbors who had passed. The sweetness of the lives blown away by time and illness resonated through her in a calmer quiet that she could take home to Lilac Hill.

Returning to the car, Sarah ran the engine for a few minutes until the heater thawed her toes; she withdrew a blanket from the back seat of the car, drank a bit of coffee from the thermos and switched off the engine. Parked on a side street on the outskirts of Trenton, New Jersey, Sarah Monroe wrapped up in a blanket and slept through most of Christmas Day while a snowstorm enveloped the East Coast.

Hours away to the south, her family read her brief note and figured she had lost some battle with loss, identity or pressure. Sarah Monroe slept until midnight, woke and drove to a truck stop on I-76 to stretch and run a few laps inside the building, cleaned off the car and came directly back. As she maneuvered through the single lane highways due to snowplows and minor accidents, she sang a little thinking about home. Home was Monroe Farm on Lilac Hill outside of Lambertville, West Virginia. Her family had expanded beyond Julie to the children, included Michael and Walt with their families; it encompassed the Lamberts, Maggie Turner, Lou and Billy. She was thrilled with the prospect of a life so deeply rich in the possibilities of love.

The morning after Christmas Day, Sarah entered the Lamberts' kitchen just a bit early for her usual four-thirty arrival. She tried not to make too much noise as she struggled to retrieve her overnight bag from the frozen trunk and crunched over the icy parking lot to the back door. She flicked on the lights but stepped back to the little room they used as a locker room with its tiny bathroom and series of bins for their belongings. Sarah hung up her coat and slipped off her boots. She opened up the overnight bag and found the new underwear, jeans and tee-shirt. She felt oddly nervous. Hopped on caffeine, she would try to make the day though her limbs were trembling from sleeping in the car, too many cups of coffee and the terrible driving conditions.

She was standing in her bra and work chinos when the door banged open and forced a yelp from her throat. Walt stepped into the small room and growled, "Get dressed." He thrust her tee-shirt at her, so she pulled it over her head.

She began to say something sarcastic, but her voice failed when she registered the same fierce anger she'd glimpsed in him on Halloween. His hair stuck out in places like he'd just awoken, and his beard had grown in a day or so. His eyes were dark with unfriendliness. So the mild, entertaining man had an edge.

Sarah nearly nodded as she gloated over pushing his limits this far. She stared up at him, and he stared down at her for about a half a minute before he bent only slightly to pick her up off her feet and throw her over his back. Sarah grunted as he knocked the wind out of her lungs, but she had the good sense not to struggle as her head narrowly missed at least two doorways. He was striding through the mansion to some destination that eluded her.

When he threw her down on a wide bed in a deserted room on the far side of the place, her eyes widened further. He tossed her overnight bag onto a chair, and she noticed that his coat hung on another chair with his boots beside it. "You stayed here last night?"

Walt nodded and pulled out his shirt from his pants and began unbuttoning it. His eyes did not invite her to protest. He stripped to his tee-shirt and shorts and said, "Take off your pants and get in bed. They expect you in the kitchen by nine. This way we might both get a little sleep before work."

"Sleep with you?" Sarah jumped up because she was shocked by his caveman approach this morning. His hand snapped out and captured her, pulled off her chinos and slammed her back down on the bed.

He held her with both arms and one leg in a smothering stranglehold, so he could growl in her ear, "Don't worry, sweet-heart. I am so tired and angry with you that you could come at me naked right now, and I wouldn't want you." He shook her just a little as he adjusted his hold to make it more comfortable for his limbs.

"I left a note. I left a message on your answering machine. I came back, Walt." In this tight hold, she was speaking directly into his neck. She sounded teary and contrite.

He raised his head, examined her face and shook his head in disgust, "You took off in a Nor'easter to visit with your dead parents. You didn't stay with any of those flirty girls you paraded around here on Thanksgiving to get rid of me. Where did you sleep? Did you sleep?" His eyes lost the burn of anger as he spoke into wide, blue eyes that shimmered with tears that would fall soon. "You didn't have to go so far to get rid of me," his voice told hurt.

"I don't want to get rid of you. You are too fine for me, Walt Stone." He continued to stare at her to get answers to his questions, "I slept in the car after a long talk with my parents. Did Jason tell you about his father?"

Walt nodded and relaxed just a bit. He had a feeling that the revelation of her parentage might have sent her over the edge. Her sister had whispered secrets of anxiety medication that Sarah had weaned out of her system during the first few months on the farm. Walt began to kiss Sarah's face gently and murmur soothing little sounds to lure her into relaxing with him. She was strung tight like piano wire. "Joseph Lambert shouldn't have done that to you. Your father will always be John Monroe, right?"

Sarah nodded and felt her heart break in half. She gulped, "In every way that matters. That's what I wanted to see; I needed to look at their names and think of them side by side my whole life—their whole lives. He was a good man just like you, Walt. I told my mother that. I am so angry with her."

Tears spilled, and Walt kissed her mouth tenderly. "I know

you are. Thing is, Sarah, you came back. I am holding you here in this bed until we both fall asleep. I am grateful that you are back." He settled her next to him and lightly rubbed her arm. "You are going to need some rest before you face the wrath of your sister and brothers. Yes, both Jason and Stephen were beside themselves. Michael and I drank enough beer not to jump in the truck and go after you. Your friends in Trenton are worried. Jason even called your lover boy Jennings just in case you went running back to Boston. I knew you'd wind up back here, but it was so hard to stay put where you left me." He shrugged away irritation. "Miss Maggie told me to stay here until we want to face them. When you do, I want you to promise all of them not to do something like that again. You just don't run away from your family. Got it?" He tightened his arms to steel bands and nudged her into place against him.

Sarah nodded and kissed Walt's neck hesitantly. He shivered, and she chuckled, "You don't do caveman well at all." She closed her eyes because his were closed though he smiled. She was asleep in his arms in less than a minute, and he enjoyed her weight against his body only a few more.

When they woke slowly hours later, she was sprawled on top of him in the effort to take up the entire bed. He ran a hand down her back and dared to touch her rear barely covered by her underwear. When his hand moved back up to fiddle with her bra straps, she sprang into a crouch and grinned down at him. "I was going to knee you if you slipped your hand into my pants."

He laughed and rolled her under him to pin her securely to the bed. He adjusted his body to fit hers even closer than the stranglehold from earlier. "If I decided to take you that far, you would have no opportunity to disable me, sweetie. Count your lucky stars that I want you the right way, the forever way." He rubbed his body against hers and made her ache.

"You are so bad."

"You don't know the half of it." He jumped up half in self-protection and glanced at the clock. He bolted into the bathroom and muttered, "I'm late for my route. I call the shower." Sarah lay back in the bed that smelled of Walt Stone and felt a purr leave her throat. She hadn't messed it all up despite her best efforts.

CHAPTER 18

Walt and the Big Rig

January brought icy roads up and down the coast. Within the mountains, the state road was usually warmed by the sun until you climbed to higher elevations. Walt Stone had driven these roads all his life and knew every turn, each climb with slipping tires and the exact spot where his defenses diminished during the last fifty miles before home. That knowledge usually perked him up enough not to fall asleep or be lulled into complacency. So he was surprised right out of singing a country tune about everlasting love that he and Sarah had danced to last week when he came around a tight curve forty miles outside of Wheeling and overturned his truck avoiding the cab of a jackknifed tractor trailer. The last thing he remembered was the horrified look on the other driver's face and the sound of a steel guitar launching into the bridge of the song.

He woke once in a daze of bright lights and cold, sleety rain, but he could still hear the song playing in an endless loop. He was relieved that he felt freezing cold and not the heat of the big rig exploding in flames. His uncle had died in a big rig accident years ago, and the gruesome tale of his fiery death was haunting.

Walt closed his eyes and fell back into the song. His whispered request was simple, "Dance with me, Sarah Monroe?" While they worked on him and his parents rushed to his side, Walt Stone danced with his elusive, fiery girl. Her hair was swept up in a twist like the first night he dared to ask her to dance. He had watched for her every evening in June, hiding behind a computer monitor in the library or following her around in the grocery store with the children. He'd thought to catch her eye in produce with a silly question about the ripeness of cantaloupe but hesitated, not wanting to seem too stupid. She was so strict with the children yet eager to laugh with them. She sounded like a little girl when she whispered to them. That's what he wanted to know better: he wanted her to laugh like that with him and break that serious frown she turned on most men.

He slept and rewrote their first dance together when she was so fragile and lonely. She had looked straight up into his face, and all he could think of was kissing her. He had blundered into embarrassment and had wanted to take it back immediately. In his new dream, he confessed that he was madly in love with her and would do anything to make her smile at him. In his dream, they danced all that evening and could only see each other in the crowded hall.

But he remembered that the real Sarah had slowly forgiven his awkwardness with her. She had even accepted his oaf-like advances in her little house. When they danced now, it was easier and companionable. Walt felt his love for Sarah bloom and grow from his chest through his abdomen and flow out to his arms, fingers and down through his thighs, knees, legs and feet. He saw her the day that she painted the trim and door of her cottage that girly lavender, and he fell further, knock-kneed in love with her.

When they drank coffee and ate ice cream later, and talked so they could be friends, he'd been thinking they could have three children like her sister did. He was imagining little children blue-eyed as Sarah or brown-eyed like him. He could imagine their hair soft on his fingers—silky, thick-tresses—raven brunettes or redheaded like his father. He felt the weight of their little bodies leaning on his like Annabelle pressed when she spoke to him about Sarah.

There was a long time of muted, cottony-cloud dreams and then he battled back to color and sound. Sound and light let ferocious pain invade his head, so he retreated in reflex. Someone spoke to him as he battled back to opening his eyes. Once he dreamed that he and Sarah dug up and moved every damned rock in her patio. Every time he lifted one of the stones, his heart hurt intolerably, and he knew it was the weight of love. Sarah would kill him with this heavy, ponderous love. So he let go of the rocks and fell back into the silt-like desire for her and swam in it like he had for months.

He was hardly surprised to see Sarah Monroe sitting next to him when he woke from an induced coma three days after the accident. He opened his hand, and she slipped her fingers into his. He examined her thin face and her worry expressed in a quivery smile before she whispered his name.

She reached over and pushed the button for the nurse. "He's awake," her voice was rough in a way he'd never heard it. She gently pushed back his shoulder as he tried to sit forward, "Walt, don't try to move yet. They want to check your reflexes and unhook all these tethers." She gestured to all the attachments that had kept him alive while he'd been out dreaming over his life.

When he tried to speak, he started to choke, and his struggle brought tears to her eyes, "They'll be in to take that out. Walt, be patient." That made her cry in earnest, and she shook her head at the alarm in his eyes. "No, you'll be fine. I can't believe I just told you to be patient when that's exactly what you've been, isn't it?" She was stroking his cheek as her tears choked her. "I have been so frightened, Walt. Please forgive me." She leaned over him, kissed his forehead and dabbed at the places where tears leaked from his eyes.

When the nurses arrived, Sarah retreated to the bottom edge of the bed but did not leave his sight. She did not turn away even when he choked over the removal of the tracheal tube. She maintained eye contact even as he lay gasping when the doctor left to phone his parents.

Sarah moved back to the chair by his side while he looked at himself fastened to the bed by lines filled with fluid. He wanted to rip them all off and sweep her up in his arms like he should have months ago. Incredible anger at his helplessness filled him while he took stock in the cast on his left leg, the taped ribs, a long bandage at his abdomen and stiffness at the back of his head he took as a bandage. His face was stitched and taped in various places. Later he would realize he'd broken an arm and numerous bones in one of his hands. His voice was the harsh one that had struggled to answer all of the nurses' questions, "Sarah Monroe, am I still whole enough to be a man for you?"

She nodded and leaned forward to touch his hand, "Yes, sweetheart. I am sorry about how stubborn I've been. I do love you, Walt."

He stared into her eyes and whispered, "I'm holding you to that. I love you back." He closed his eyes and concentrated on the giddy happiness that spread through his body despite the pain.

CHAPTER 19

The Thaw

"Are you marrying that man you kidnapped from the hospital?" Maggie was back to being moody and acerbic toward Sarah and the rest of humanity. Sarah figured that Maggie knew they had the DNA test results and that Isabel felt hurt all over again. Isabel thought her husband set the whole mess up, especially considering that Joseph Lambert had sold John Monroe the farm at Lilac Hill. Joseph had put Sarah in their midst and waited to see if they'd figure it out. Isabel could not quite forgive Joseph because he'd hinted at Sarah's identity for months while she worked in their kitchen. Though Isabel had dissolved into anxiety attacks and illness, her husband persisted in manipulating all of them by holding back the truth.

Isabel and Sarah had walked out to the fire line and back in a light snow just after Walt was released from the hospital. Isabel wanted to discuss the circumstances surrounding Sarah's conception. Isabel told her hilarious stories of parties the couples threw together, spontaneous picnics and midnight skinny-dipping. Sarah privately thought that shedding clothes was nearly always a precursor to naughtiness. Sarah wondered if Isabel and John Monroe had liked each other also. Isabel's fond remembrances had tarnished the shiny, saint-like images of both John and Elizabeth Monroe. Instead of feeling disappointed like Julie, Sarah felt something unravel and relax just a little bit.

The morning that Maggie's question about marriage rocketed through the quiet kitchen, Sarah felt confused, "I think I would if he asked, but he hasn't, Miss Maggie. It's not like we're living in sin." She giggled over it because she was likely to sin if he stayed much longer than the four weeks he'd been there. His parents had taken a cross-country trip they'd delayed after the accident. If Walt stayed at Lilac Hill, there was at least one of three adults and three children within shouting distance twenty-four hours a day. In truth, if he wanted to return to his Lambertville house, Sarah knew she'd go with him.

That assertion made Maggie laugh out loud, "Poor man! Walt must be miserable! Did I ever tell you that Walt Stone used to shoot birds out at your farm?" She sobered up as she said it.

Sarah gave the old woman a quizzical look, "You have told me twice. Is that fact supposed to be significant?" Sarah was suspicious of the weird, coded language between the Lamberts and their employees. Sarah looked at Maggie Turner and wondered what else she knew about the past that hovered unsaid like parentage, the idiosyncrasies of marriage and the weakness of human nature.

Sarah had tried on the green gown from the old wardrobe on an impulse the previous night, and her appearance had made Walt catch his breath. She'd pinned up her hair and donned the white gloves just to serve him dinner at her old rough table. He had pulled her down beside him though it pulled his bandages. They leaned together for a few minutes of kissing before she retrieved the potatoes. He had turned surly and quiet, so she'd taken the gown off before they ate pie by the fire in the woodstove Michael had just installed.

Maggie shook her head, "I just want you to remember to ask about it, Sarah." She waved a knife in the air, "Your mother? Pretty Elizabeth Walden Monroe? She was my older brother Paul's daughter. You and I are related, Sarah. I do feel protective of you." She began cutting the meat before her carefully though her hands were shaking.

Sarah bit her lip then asked slowly, "Why didn't you tell me before now? Is it hurtful?"

Maggie nodded and continued to make her precise cuts. She finally looked up to Sarah's hard eyes on her, "I like you far more than any kin I've ever known, Sarah. It's your fault that I love you." Sarah nodded back with sudden tears in her eyes, but then Maggie waved the knife and chilled Sarah, "You ask that Walter about killing birds at your farm before you marry him. Okay?"

Sarah agreed seriously, "I will. If I'm not satisfied with his story, we'll be honest about this, right? Whatever it is, we'll clear it up?"

Maggie nodded and went back to making the meal with quiet determination. Sarah wondered if the man she'd convinced herself that she loved was a stranger or her friend.

Jason Lambert was confused by his feelings for Sarah Monroe. He knew he fell in love with her the first time she'd snapped at him at the playground. He'd told himself that he wanted to protect her from the same mistakes that had caused the accident that killed his wife. She had confounded him with her silence and pretense of docility. He had pressed her into the role of auditor to battle her impenetrable reserve. When he discovered that she was simply an over-sensitive, highly intelligent girl with no promiscuous past, he'd been oddly deflated. She might have been his Mary Magdalene to save and cherish before Michael Elliott was revealed her brother-in-law. Two kisses between them, and he hoped she would make demands, run away or find another man.

His father had driven the final wedge between them with his claim as her father. Jason thought it spoke best of her that she did not embrace the idea in any way. She loved John Monroe as her father and a model of the person she aspired to become. She had asked for the DNA test to squash any claim his father might have on her.

Jason Lambert examined himself in the mirror one morning and wondered why he had let three years expire without erasing the scars from the accident. While Walt Stone was convalescing at Monroe Farm with Sarah, Jason asked her to keep an eye on Chloe, so he could traveled to New York to see the plastic surgeons. Sarah Monroe had shaken him out of complacency; half-sister and friend, he loved Sarah for tumbling him out of his comfortable, warped world.

Sarah returned to Monroe Farm every evening to find some little part of the cottage improved while Walt Stone convalesced there. He was supposed to be resting and healing, but he fixed screens, cleaned windows, and made a bank of book shelves for her collection of texts housed in ugly plastic crates. The man was as good at resting as she was. He had started to refinish a headboard and footboard that Michael found in the barn. His efforts would make her bed into a four-poster luxury. He sanded and smoothed on the varnish, sanded again the next day and varnished again.

Sarah would often arrive home, shower and change without speaking to him. She would pour him a drink and get herself one to sip as he finished the task he'd chosen for the day. Only after he glanced at her and smiled would she approach him to run a hand over his back or through his dark hair. Then they would talk about the day, the weather, Julie's children, news from friends or other excuses to trade information and odd stories. They needed to thaw out every day after being parted.

During dinner preparation, the kissing could begin. Walt liked to chop, he could grate, and most importantly, he wanted to be right there and part of the meal unlike anyone she'd known. She would help him clean up afterward with bathing that was achy and thrilling in its intimacy. Sometimes his eyes would tear, and she would ask him if it hurt. He might nod or shrug. Once he muttered, "I just love you too much."

They lay in bed together every night before she slid out to sleep on the divan. All night made them both fractious and led to a number of arguments that were nothing but frustration. In bright daylight, they could laugh about it, but the nights were torture with touching but not having; it was miserable.

On the evening that Maggie had been so insistent, Sarah waited until they were lying together to ask Walt about shooting birds at the farm. "Maggie says you shot birds out here when you were younger, Walt. Why is she so odd about it?" Sarah was running a hand over his chest and riffling his hairs that curled tightly. The man's broad chest made her weak.

Walt shifted to look at Sarah directly and asked for a lullaby, "Tell me again what you felt when I kissed you on this bed in October. I never knew, Sarah. I thought I messed it all up with you again." He made little circles with his thumb on her collarbone.

Sarah's mouth pursed into a bit of a smirk, "Like melted chocolate, I told you Walt. I never admitted it, but that night, I ran on the frozen track until the whole path melted to mud. I wanted you back all that weekend, Walt Stone." Sarah pushed herself up to lean over him for a steadily warming kiss.

Walt groaned under such attention, "Oh, my lovely Sarah. I hoped you'd come to love me." He sighed and made her. He settled her with her face resting on his bare arm. Her arm and hand was draped over his chest. He took a deep breath and admitted, "I used to come out here and hunt with Mr. Walden. My dad used to bring me out, and then later, I came on my own. After Mr. Walden died, Miss Maggie caught me out here in the house with a woman. I was seventeen. She didn't like it, kicked me off the place and told me not to come back. I never did until Julie moved back here with the kids."

"So in her mind, you were trespassing and possibly having a bit of a romance," it unsettled her a bit, but he'd been young and probably full of himself like the first night they'd danced together. She thought about the green dress upstairs and blushed.

Walt stiffened under her touch when her hand slid down to his belly. His abdomen was taut remembering, "Sarah, it wasn't just a girl; Miss Maggie stopped me from having sex for the first time with a woman—a woman who had keys to the place. I'd never break into Mr. Walden's place." He shifted to tip up Sarah's chin, so she looked right at him.

"Sarah, I was going to bed with Annette Lambert."

Sarah was confused at this revelation. She didn't know an Annette among the family. She thought about his age and counted back in time to another era for the Lamberts. Her body stiffened as she realized why this might bother Maggie, "Jason Lambert's wife? Why would she be unfaithful? They must have just been married!" She pushed up on one elbow and looked at him carefully. She was trying to imagine Walt as a boy. He suddenly seemed older than his thirties as he looked at her.

Walt nodded, "They got married right out of college. She was twenty-one and so worldly. She was beautiful like Chloe is. Annette was small and blonde with big breasts that she stuck out and dared me to touch. What can I say? I put down the rifle and accommodated her." He sighed, "When Miss Maggie surprised us in the house, Annette tried to say I forced her; it was a nightmare. Maggie aimed my rifle at both of us and threatened to kill either of us if we ever told. She escorted me off the property, unloaded the gun and threw it into the back of my truck. Not long after, I heard that Annette and Jason moved back to New York."

Sarah nodded understanding Maggie's concern over Sarah caring for this man in a cottage where he'd betrayed Jason, a man Maggie loved like a son. Sarah's heart ached over Jason yet again. She wished he could find some happiness. No wonder Jason had a patented distrust of young women like her.

Walt stroked her hair as she thought about it. He felt relieved that she didn't act self-righteous about the incident like he expected. When he thought Jason Lambert was interested in Sarah last summer, Walt had backed off half out of guilt.

Sarah looked at Walt steadily but continued to stroke his chest, "Walt, did Jason ever find out?" She thought about Jason's words months ago about Walt being a good guy. Jason's generosity was endless.

Walt groaned at the memory but admitted, "I told my father what happened that day. He worked for the Lamberts from time to time, and I was worried it would hurt him. I felt so stupid. He and I visited Jason and Joseph Lambert together in the office at the mansion. It taught me a real lesson about how good men handle themselves. Jason was horrified, but his father calmed him down and put it in perspective. Years later, the Lamberts actually helped finance me when I wanted to take over the distributorship." He closed his eyes as tension left both of them.

Sarah tapped on Walt's chest, "So how many women have

you coerced into bed, Mr. Stone? I might as well know where I stand." She kissed his chin a bit annoyed with asking.

Walt thought for a moment about how to answer her. Lying would be too easy, so he took the high road and uttered the truth, "I have had three serious girlfriends."

Sarah sighed heavily, "Am I number three or four? Gee, Walt, I hope I count as serious." Now her throat was full of tears as she considered her fear and inexperience. His convalescence had made their bond artificially close.

Walt hugged her tight to his chest and kissed her neck, "You, my love, are not a serious girlfriend. I have been married to you since you rescued Annabelle from that jungle gym the night of the movies. I watched you climb that thing with my heart beating so fast, all I could do was stare. Do you know how many times I've wanted to scoop you up and take you home? I love you. Could we please get married, Sarah?"

She giggled at his rendition of an evening she had only remembered in irritation with Jason. Her mouth found his and answered, "Yes" on whispered kisses.

Walt smiled after she turned off the light but stayed beside him in the dark, "So what number lover am I?" He felt the most fortunate man on earth.

Sarah was silent for a moment, and he feared she misunderstood, "If you don't want to talk about it, Sarah. I was just . . ."

She shook her head and put her fingers on his lips which he kissed gently. "Other than kisses, you are really the only man I've allowed this close to me. I do love you. I wouldn't say it lightly, Walt."

Walt let his worries evaporate over loving Sarah Monroe. He fell asleep lulled into dreaming of children and dancing with his fiery girl.

AFTERWORD

Dance on the Patio

They were slow dancing under a moonlit sky that only shines after the winter cold. In early spring, the air is scrubbed clean, and the stars show so clearly they look painted. Her dad, the John Monroe father, told her that the cold made the air like crystal in the mountains, so the stars and moon appeared closer and brighter. She remembered the velvet blue night of late May before her first thunderstorm on Lilac Hill and marveled that it was the same sky. So much on earth, so much on Lilac Hill, had changed.

Sarah moved her head to try to look at the visage of the man holding her loosely. He no longer clutched her too close, and she could now comfortably look up at him when they danced in town. He had become accustomed to the distance that she needed to see him properly. Perhaps he now felt confident that she would not slip away. She had slid her hand into his four months ago and had promised to hold on tight. And she had. Sarah could not imagine a next step under the night sky or the wide, searching blue of morning without him.

Even with the moon lighting the stone patio they had built and with which they measured and weighed their regard for each other in damp December, Sarah could only see Walt in an outline. He was a large man who didn't seek to be imposing because he simply was tall and wide-shouldered. His face looking down to hers was a mask of shadows. She shivered because he looked like a stranger again in that moment.

"Cold?" he resisted the urge to stop dancing and hug her close or let his mouth graze hers. This was his dream since meeting her when she was too young to understand deep love. Who was he kidding? He hadn't understood it himself. But he did comprehend the urge to protect this woman and everyone she loved. And she did the same for him without prodding.

Sarah stepped closer to him though she shook her head,

"I wanted to see your face. It is so dark, and the sky is crispy clear." She grinned at putting it so badly.

Walt allowed himself to step a bit closer and brush his mouth and cheek over her face. "My dad always says it's the cold. Clears the air and lets us glimpse heaven."

Sarah stood on tiptoes to brush her returning kiss on his mouth as an invitation. "My father used to say the same thing. Walt, do you remember the first time we met?"

"In May? You were walking with the kids after church all dolled up in that pretty summer dress. You had that Audrey Hepburn—I-just-walked-off-the-Champs de Elyse thing going on. If I hadn't just come back from a fishing trip, I'd have fallen down on the sidewalk and proposed then. I should have." Walt was still reeling from her turnabout rush to return his affections by the end of that year. She'd spent most of her first few months telling him to get lost without being too rude. The fleeting pain of that rejection made his mouth seek hers for a real kiss that stopped the dancing momentarily.

When the kissing ended, Sarah didn't even take a breath, "Oh that day! That was the day I thought you looked like a magazine model for bad boys. You know; you were doing the rough-cheeked cowboy look." She lifted one hand so her fingers could touch his after-four growth. His whiskers on her fingers caused a tickle in her belly. If he hadn't been such a good man, a kind and patient man, she might have rejected her quivery reaction to his proximity as hormones. But she'd tested it, and this thing with Walt was all tied up with being his friend.

Walt offered a bit of distance and swung her back into the dancing. He had closed his eyes to the bright night sky just to enjoy the feeling of her in his arms. He grinned at how much pleasure it gave him. Her voice started again, "No, Walt. The first time we met was at Julie's wedding in Wheeling. You were standing up for Michael and came in with a note for Julie that Michael was too superstitious to deliver. I met you the night before, but I thought you were a drunken lout trying to lure Julie out on the porch for kisses." In the dark, her voice contained sharp chiding.

Walt thought about the odd weekend four years ago when Michael called to say he'd convinced the pretty bookkeeper he'd been dating to marry him. He'd asked Walt to stay with him for the usual party the night before the wedding with a bit of drinking and carousing. Walt had been surprised at how settled his old friend had been with the idea of marriage to the gorgeous woman with two little children. All of their friends had figured Michael would slip away before any girl could get a ring on his hand. After a few drinks that night, all Michael really wanted was Julie. He was such a sad-sack about it that Walt had agreed to drive him to her cousin's house where they were staying.

How could he forget his first glimpse of Sarah Monroe? It had been late, but she'd still been dressed in a little skirt and a sweater like she had arriving there that afternoon. She'd been hemming the dress she'd bought her sister for the surprise wedding from a department store sale in Boston. When he first saw her, Sarah had straight pins stuck in one sleeve of her sweater and a spool of pale pink thread in her hand. Her hair had been falling out of the quick ponytail she'd twisted behind her, and her eyes had been large and tired as they blinked to adjust to the porch light. "Yes? Everyone is asleep here. Michael Elliott, just what are you up to so late?" Her hands had crept up to her hips when she realized he was swaying with inebriation. Walt and two of their oldest friends hung back in the shadows at the bottom of the stairs chuckling.

Michael had smiled in his bemused way, "Oh my, Sarah Monroe! I'm glad that you've come from Boston. I'm here for a kiss from your lovely sister. But come here and meet my best friends. Walt, Bobby and Joe, this beautiful creature is Julie's little sister." He waved them into the house with Sarah shushing them briskly and leading them into the kitchen. The pink ghost of Julie hung in the living room where Sarah had been finishing alterations. They made more noise in the exaggeration of staying quiet than four large men shuffling through a house normally made. Sarah arched a brow and said, "I'm making a pot of coffee while Michael gets his kiss. Who's driving tonight?"

Walt had stepped forward without thinking, and she had put the first coffee cup in front of him. "You get two cups of coffee." Then she had grinned up into his face and had stopped his heart the first of many times. He'd looked at her in bemusement and had thought he'd like kisses from her lips.

Just to keep her interest, he'd flirted, "I'd rather have two kisses from you." Her eyes had darkened, but she had stretched her arms and rolled her shoulders in an innocently provocative movement. All three men stared at her, and Joe licked his lips.

She shook her head and crossed the room to withdraw milk and find the sugar bowl, "What a bunch of flirts. I take it you didn't do the required stripper thing?" These men were old enough to be uncles or older brothers in her mind; they were Michael's friends and harmless.

Joe laughed at that and shook his head. Bobby muttered, "No, my wife would kill me." Sarah poured them cups of steaming coffee and half-filled one for herself. She sat in the chair nearest Walt and fixed her cup with lots of milk. Her eyes flashed at Walt's amusement over her generosity with the milk.

She had smiled at him again and made his insides quake. She raised the mug to the three men and offered, "To Michael and Julie, harmless kisses and coffee at midnight!" They toasted with good-hearted grins, but Joe and Bobby gasped as she leaned over to Walt and gave him a light kiss on the cheek. He turned his face automatically and took another on her mouth with his lips. Her eyes were open and filled with laughter. "Nice to meet you, Walt," she purred.

Walt had shaken his head ruefully, "Nice to meet you, Sarah Monroe."

The next morning had been a whirl of hysteria over dressing, hair and makeup. Julie had been beset with nerves, worrying about making a bad decision. The reverend came into the little room they were using to primp the last time and said a man wanted to see the bride.

When Walt had come into the vestment room of the little church, Sarah had nearly barred his way. He'd had half a desire to wipe the smirk from her face; she figured they were all hung-over. "I have a note from Michael for Julie." He knew his voice was rougher than normal because the sight of her in the short, rose-colored gown made him choke. With her dark hair twisted up and a careful diamond clip on one side, her blue eyes seemed wider and softer than last evening. "Sarah, you look incredible."

She gracefully blushed at his approval and took the note, "Does he want to back out of the wedding?"

Walt had laughed in a snort, "No! I've never seen him like this. No, he's all romance and moonlight. How is Julie?" He smiled down to a little girl who was suddenly clinging to Sarah.

Sarah touched the little girl's cheek and gave the note to her, "Give this to your Mommy right away." The little girl was wearing a miniature version of the dress that hugged Sarah's curves. Sarah looked up into Walt's open curiosity, "Julie is nervous, but she's excited nervous. Ten minutes?"

Walt nodded and turned to leave her there at the door guarding all the female shenanigans with last minute repairs to makeup and hair. He looked back and found her lounging in the doorway watching him walk away. His smile made her blush.

Walt held Sarah on their stone patio four years later and felt his heart grow heavy in his chest. He had suffered a little bit to earn his dance partner. He remembered Michael's romantic impulses over Julie before their wedding. He understood the acceptance necessary to mate with another human for life. Yes, there was love and desire, but sometimes there was aggravation and hurt. Weathering all those changes was required to earn this partner. His mouth brushed her cheek, "I love you, Sarah Monroe." His voice was that rough one that told desire.

Sarah moved her face to capture his mouth with hers. Her hand left his shoulder and brushed his cheek in the dark, "You remembered our first kiss. I thought you were drunk." They stopped dancing.

He cupped her face in his hands, "Sweetheart, thank you for letting me get over being a fool. I've spent a long time flirting and carousing just like you thought when we first met. I think I had to live like that to be ready for us. You tickled me even that first night. Bobby and Joe teased me about being a goner all that next day. I'm sorry I was so awkward." He held her close just like she wanted him to do.

She rested her head on his chest and felt the rapid thumping of his heart. She was grateful for that steady heartbeat and hugged him back. "Walt, that's part of what I wanted you to remember. I wasn't ready for you either. I was just so relieved that Julie found someone as fine as Michael. She's a woman who needs a man all the time to lean on and share the load. I had to go back to Boston and finish what I'd started. It was a hole in my life. I needed to struggle here with Julie, the children, this dilapidated farm, the job with the Lamberts, even the CPA exam just to grow up the rest of the way to get ready for you." She stroked his cheek and brushed her fingers over his lips. "I love you. I love you in every part of my body, every thought, each dream. Everything in my life has led me to you over and over again. Sometimes I think I'm so dumb, I needed you to keeping insisting like you did, so I'd wake up."

Walt laughed, "That day in the barber shop when you suggested I shave off my sideburns, I nearly pulled you into my lap right there. You gave me hope that day, Sarah." He felt her shiver as she moved her fingers along his cheek where the rough hairs were bristling. "You are one independent, prickly girl, but I don't think I'd want you any other way." His hand cupped her chin and tilted her face up to his for another gentle touch, "So are you going to marry me tomorrow, sweetheart?"

"Yes, Walt. Of course I will marry you." She stood on tiptoes to start the kiss under the descending stars burning so bright on the blue velvet sky above Lilac Hill. Sarah felt the gladness rising up from the stones that they'd laid themselves, the shiver of the pines in the forest surrounding them and the echoes of love pouring up from the valley nestled in the bowl of the earth. If she could stay wrapped in his arms for all eternity right in this spot, all rips in time, heartaches ages old, and mistakes of being human could be healed. She felt herself growing warm and full in his arms; she understood that the recuperation she desired had begun.

About The Author

Joan D. Cooper moved to Maryland's Eastern Shore ten years ago and shifted from writing poetry to spinning fiction. A career educator, she finds inspiration in her three children, extended family, lifelong friends and two rambunctious dogs. Member of the *Eastern Shore Writer's Association*, advisor for *Poetry Out Loud* and patron of Brown Box Theatre Project's *Free Shakespeare at the Beach* initiative, she is committed to teaching and writing. Contact her at joandcooper.com for other projects and a creative writing blog.

Stories from Lilac Hill continues the Lilac Hill narrative through three, connected novellas.